PALEO DIET

COOKBOOK FOR BEGINNERS

1500-Days of Tasty & Quick Recipes with Easy-to-Find Ingredients, to Lose Weight and Achieve the Healthy Lifestyle of our Ancestors, Including a 30-Day Meal Plan

Emily Young

TABLE OF CONTENTS

Introduction

The paleo diet is eating that is concentrating on foods that our caveman ancestors would have eaten. It is a relatively simple diet, but it does require quite a bit of work. You need to eat unprocessed foods, limit your salt intake, eat healthy fats, and eat some fruit.

It allows you to avoid foods that have been associated with the disease. It helps reduce food cravings as it doesn't contain processed food full of sugar, fat, and carbs. It helps you to make better decisions as you can be more in tune with your body's needs. It is a low-carb, high protein diet, so it aids in weight loss and muscle gain. It is high in fat, so it suppresses hunger while providing energy for your body.

The paleo diet has several benefits for you. It is a very healthy diet that can help improve your body's overall health because you are not eating processed foods. Your diet will also help you look better and feel better as it removes junk food from your system.

Using the paleo diet cookbook can help you stick to the diet for the long term. All recipes are made with easy ingredients that focus on whole foods as opposed to processed products. As a bonus, all recipes are gluten-free! The paleo diet is appraised by many to be a healthy and balanced eating plan. This diet is based on the reliance that our body was meant to eat foods naturally. It primarily focuses on whole foods like fruits, vegetables, nuts, and seeds rather than processed foods to supply all of the necessary vitamins, minerals, and other nutrients to maintain and improve your health.

The paleo diet has been obtaining popularity over the last few years, especially among those interested in losing weight and enhance their overall health. Many people believe that this eating plan helps achieve both of those goals. The paleo diet cookbook is designed for beginners who are new to this eating plan.

The paleo diet encourages consuming whole foods with minimal processing or cooking. You can enjoy foods like meats, kinds of seafood, eggs, fruits, vegetables, and nuts without the addition of oils or other unhealthy additives. The paleo diet adopts high-fiber consumption and plenty of fruits and vegetables to help you stay healthy and fit. The paleo diet is a program that focuses on eating like it did in the Paleolithic Era. The paleo diet's mantra is that humans have an innate tendency to eat like our hunter-gatherer ancestors.

The paleo diet is constructed on the idea that modern man has become out-of-sync with his physiology. This out-of-sync can be attributed to the introduction of agriculture in the Neolithic era, which displaced our ancient hunter-gatherer ancestors. The theory goes that modern man is no longer fulfilling his physical requirements for food.

Many people of all ages have adopted this eating pattern out of a desire to lose weight and feel healthier and get a boost in their energy levels. Whether you want to drop a couple of pounds or you want a healthier lifestyle, paleo diet cookbooks can help you on your way. Throughout history, our ancient ancestors were hunters and gatherers. They spent their days searching for food and gathering around campfires to share stories and survival tips. They did not have access to modern conveniences such as farming or cooking, so they were highly selective about what they ate. Their food choices were built on what was available at the time, whether it was safe to eat or tasted good. This is why we see many similarities between paleo diet principles and eating habits among our ancient ancestors.

Today, we gather most of our days indoors and in front of computer screens. Taking care of business means having access to many different types of food during the day, but when you're Paleo, you are only allowed to eat foods that were available to our ancient ancestors. Due to this reason alone, many people believe that the Paleo Diet is an effective way to lose weight or gaining a healthy lifestyle. Many people who follow this diet have claimed that it helped relieve joint pain, balance blood sugar levels, lower cholesterol levels, and even help with allergies.

It's a diet that utilizes the foods that our ancestors ate and eliminates the foods they didn't. The paleo diet uses healthy grains, nuts, and meat along with vegetables. It also excludes dairy. The basic idea behind Paleo is to eat whole foods and avoid processed foods.

This is a guide for people that are looking for a dietary change that can benefit their health. It takes you step by step to follow the paleo diet, including how to choose paleo-friendly foods. We've included recipes for every meal, so you can easily find tasty dishes to fit this diet. We've even included tips on cooking the most popular recipes in the paleo cookbook so you can prepare your meals right at home. The recipes are available in print or for download as PDFs, which means that you'll be ready to go at a moment's notice!

If you're looking for a way to change up your dietary routine, this paleo cookbook has what you need! Stock up now and have a tastier way of eating soon!

CHAPTER 1

Benefits of Paleo Diet

The paleo diet plan is a diet program that mimics how pre-historic people could have eaten. It entails consuming whole food items that people could search for or collect.

Promoters from the paleo diet plan decline new diet programs that are usually filled with processed food items. They think that time for how hunter-gatherers consumed could cause fewer health issues.

The paleo diet plan isn't safe for everybody. Physicians have no idea of its results on kids, women that are pregnant, or old grownups. Individuals with persistent problems, such as inflammatory intestinal illness, should talk to a physician before trying a paleo diet plan. This manual explores paleo principles, and a 7-day paleo diet meal intends to follow. Please continue reading to understand how to consume like our forefathers. The paleo diet plan's focus is on eating foodstuffs that might have already been obtainable in the Paleolithic era. Furthermore, the paleo diet plan will be referred to as the rock age group diet plan, hunter-gatherer diet plan, or caveman diet plan. Before contemporary agriculture developed around 10,000 years back, people usually ate foods they could hunt or gather, such as fish, liver organs, fruits, vegetables, peanuts, and seeds. The introduction of modern farming changed how people ate. Milk products, dried beans, and grains grew to become a section of people's diet plans.

Advocates from the paleo diet plan believe that the body hasn't evolved to procedure dairy products, dried beans, and grains that feed on these food types could raise the threat of specific health issues, such as cardiovascular disease, being overweight, and diabetes.

Health advantages of paleo

Individuals declare that the paleo diet plan gives numerous health advantages, such as promoting weight reduction, reducing the chance of diabetes, and decreasing blood pressure. In this area, we go through the scientific evidence to find out what the study facilitates these claims:

Excess weight loss

A mature 2008 research discovered that 14 healthy volunteers achieved the average weight reduction of 2.3 kilos by following a paleo diet plan for three weeks.

In 2009, researchers compared the paleo diet plan's consequences with the diet plan for diabetes on 13 people with type 2 diabetes. Little research discovered that consuming the paleo method decreased individuals' body weight and waistline area. The 2014 research of 70 post-menopausal ladies with weight problems discovered that carrying out a paleo diet plan helped individuals shed weight after six months.

Nevertheless, right after 24 months, there has been simply no difference in weight reduction among individuals following a paleo diet and the ones sticking with regular Nordic nutritional suggestions. These outcomes claim that some other healthy diet programs could be as effective at advertising weight reduction.

The authors of the 2017 review noted that this paleo diet plan helped reduce weight for a while but figured this result is because of caloric restriction or consuming fewer calories. Generally, the study shows that the paleo diet plan can help people shed weight initially, but that additional diet plans that reduce calorie consumption might be effective. Even more, the study is essential before physicians recommend the paleo diet plan for weight reduction. Presently, physicians recommend visitors to follow a calorie-controlled exercise and diet even more to lose excess weight.

Decreasing diabetes risk

Carrying out a paleo diet program reduces one's danger of building diabetes? The outcomes of some preliminary research are usually encouraging. Insulin level of resistance is a dangerous element for diabetes. Improving one's insulin level of sensitivity reduces the probability that they can lead to diabetes and help those who have diabetes decrease their signs and symptoms. A study in 2015 compared the consequences from the paleo diet plan with those of a diet plan predicated on recommendations from your American Diabetes Association on people who have type 2 diabetes. While both diet programs improved the individuals' metabolic health, the paleo diet plan improved the insulin level of resistance and blood sugar levels control. A 2009 research of nine sedentary volunteers without obesity discovered that the paleo diet plan improved insulin awareness.

There's a requirement for a more recent study for the paleo diet plan and diabetes. However, the evidence up to now shows that eating just like a hunter-gatherer may improve insulin sensitivity.

Decreasing blood circulation pressure

Increased blood pressure is a prospect factor for cardiovascular disease. Many people believe that the paleo diet plan can help maintain bloodstream pressure in balance and advertise coronary heart wellness.

A 2008 research of 14 healthy volunteers discovered that following a paleo diet plan for 3 weeks improved systolic blood circulation pressure. It furthermore reduced excess weight and whole body bulk catalog (BMI). The analysis does not add a handle team, and nevertheless, the outcomes are usually not conclusive. The 2014 research supported these early results. Experts in comparing the consequences from the paleo diet plan with those of a diet plan the Netherlander Wellness Authorities recommend on 34 individuals with features of metabolic symptoms, a disorder that escalates the danger of cardiovascular disease.

Outcomes showed how the paleo diet plan reduced blood circulation pressure and bloodstream lipid user profile, both of which may improve center wellness.

Although preliminary studies claim that the paleo diet may reduce blood circulation pressure and support heart health, newer and considerable studies are essential to creating conclusions.

CHAPTER 2

What To Eat And What To Avoid

The Paleo diet is considered a natural way of dieting to help fuel and energize your body by supplying proteins and healthy fats while keeping lifestyle diseases at bay. The diet is comprised of a limited quantity of carbs and no processed foods at all, both of which form the bulk of the standard American diet.

On a Paleo diet, you eliminate all inflammatory or "toxic foods" and instead adopt high protein and low-fat foods such as game meat alongside fruits, veggies, eggs, seeds, and nuts. While eating raw, unprocessed, or unmodified, these foods help improve your general health.

Let's see the list of allowed foods in Paleo:

1. Lean Meats and Eggs

While meat is top of the list on paleo, you should only buy fresh grass-fed, free-range meats and poultry. Avoid marinated, batter-coated, or breaded variety. To be more specific, you are free to eat the following meat sources:

- Turkey
- Ostrich
- Quail
- Wild boar
- Turtle
- Pheasant
- Buffalo
- Rabbit
- Elk

- Goose
- Pork
- Goat
- Chicken
- Bison
- Bacon
- Grass-fed beef, ground beef, and beef jerky
- Lamb
- Organically reared eggs

2. Fish and Sea Food

Fish is rich in omega 3 fatty acids and other nutrients and thus serves as a good Paleo diet choice.

The following are the recommended fish and sea protein foods:

- Salmon
- Shrimp
- Sunfish
- Tuna
- Crawfish

- Bass
- Halibut
- Tilapia
- Shark
- Mackerel

- Lobster
- Oysters
- Crab
- Sardines
- Red snapper

- Swordfish
- Trout
- Crayfish
- Clams
- Scallops

3. Fresh Fruits and Vegetables

Make sure to buy organically grown fruits and veggies as these are free from pesticides, hormones, and chemical fertilizers. Also, avoid genetically modified produce or processed varieties in packages unless certified or natural, or organic. Ensure that farms, which produce these plant-based foods, follow the correct farming rules and no chemicals are used.

When it comes to veggies, go for non-starchy options such as:

- Watermelon
- Zucchini
- Peppers
- Brussels sprouts
- Eggplant
- Carrots
- Broccoli
- Cabbage

- Cantaloupe
- Parsley
- Green onions
- Asparagus
- Celery
- Cauliflower
- Spinach
- Artichoke hearts

Note: About starchy vegetables

The following starchy vegetables have high carb content. As such, they can easily make you gain weight, especially if you take them in excess. As such, a rule of thumb, make sure to eat these in moderation.

- Yucca
- Beets
- Potatoes
- Butternut squash
- Yam
- Acorn squash

Fruits

While fruits are nutritious and satiating, be aware that they contain fructose, a type of sugar that can lead to weight gain. Therefore, it's not advisable to over-indulge in fruits; somewhat, limit your intake to around 1-2 fruit servings daily. More precisely, to increase your odds of losing weight, it is best to focus on low-glycemic fruits such as:

- Pineapple guava
- Raspberries
- Blackberries
- Strawberries
- Mango
- Oranges
- Apple
- Lime
- Blueberries
- Avocado

- Lemon
- Peaches
- Figs
- Papaya
- Plums
- Cantaloupe
- Grapes
- Tangerine

4. Seeds and Nuts

These are rich in healthy fats and omega-3 fatty acids, but it's advisable to limit their intake. Why is that so? For starters, although they are high in fats, they also tend to be high in carbohydrates. High carb content can stall your weight loss goals, especially if you take nuts in excess.

Moreover, nuts such as cashews contain a higher amount of fats, which may hamper your weight loss goal. For this reason, try to lower the number of nuts and seeds to facilitate weight loss and healthy life.

You can eat the following:

- Pecans
- Macadamia nuts
- Cashews
- Hazelnuts
- Walnuts

- Pine nuts
- Sunflower seeds
- Flaxseeds
- Almonds
- Pumpkin seeds

5. Healthy Fats and Oils

Paleo diet is high in proteins and low in fats; therefore, limit your consumption to only those healthy or unsaturated fats and oils. Thus, aim to take fats and oils rich in omega 3 fatty acids from sources like salmon, tuna, and trout.

Here you have options such as:

- Olive oil
- Ghee

- Avocados
- Egg yolks

- Coconut oil
- Chicken fat
- Fish oil

- Macadamia oil
- Avocado oil
- Macadamia nuts

In a paleo diet, you'll need to do away with foods such as grains, wheat, soft drinks, fruit juice, among others, which can be a big challenge. Therefore, if you find it hard to cut out these foods from your diet all at once, try to reduce the amount you consume until well adapted gradually. It is easier to handle diet change in slow transitions over the long term; otherwise, you might lose motivation to stick to the diet.

Let's now see the list of foods that you should gradually eliminate from your diet.

What to Avoid

Avoid these foods:

1. Grains

Foods such as grains are considered unhealthy since they take longer to digest and often yield inflammatory byproducts. Furthermore, their absorption is still lacking, and thus their nutritional benefit is very little compared to lean protein or healthy fats. Grains also have an active ingredient referred to as lection, which can hamper other nutrients' absorption and make them counterproductive to your diet.

For that reason, avoid all foods that have grain in them, whether whole-grain, processed, or whatever kind of grains you can come across. These grains and processed wheat products include:

- Pancakes
- Crackers
- Bread
- English muffins
- Cream of wheat
- Corn
- Sandwiches
- High-fructose corn syrup

- Cakes
- Cereals
- Cookies
- Hash browns
- Lasagna
- Wheat thins
- Toast

2. Legumes

Beans, peas, and lentils aren't paleo-friendly due to their high starch (carb) content. In place of legumes, consume grass-fed animal proteins such as meat, pork, and poultry. It would be best if you steer clear of all types of beans and peas, along with peanuts and other legumes-related products.

More precisely, avoid:

- All kinds of peas
- Green beans
- White beans
- Lentils

- Soybeans
- Tofu
- Horse beans
- Lima beans

- Red beans
- String beans
- Kidney beans

- Black beans
- Broad beans
- Garbanzo beans

2. Processed Snacks and Meats:

Be aware that fast foods, processed snacks, and salty foods aren't paleo-friendly. Furthermore, artificial sweeteners aren't allowed unless in minimal amounts of organic honey, stevia, or maple syrup.

To be more specific, avoid:

- Added-salt foods
- Imitation meat
- Chips
- Pretzels
- Sauces
- Processed meats
- Seasoned snack foods

- Soups
- Salad dressings
- Hot dogs
- French fries
- Ketchup
- Cookies

3. Dairy Products

If you're lactose intolerant, you shouldn't take the milk and, if you must, ensure you consume it raw. To make your transition easier, look for alternative dairy substitutes such as almond or coconut milk, healthy and as tasty as ordinary milk.

Avoid these dairy products:

- Cheese
- Butter
- Pudding
- Whole milk Cream cheese
- Ice milk
- Ice cream
- Frozen yogurt

- Powdered milk
- Low-fat milk
- Non-fat dairy creamer
- 2% milk
- Dairy spreads
- Cottage cheese
- Skim milk

Note: However, you are free to take ghee. While it is made from dairy, many paleo experts agree that ghee doesn't contain the same properties as the other dairy products, as it is made in a process that separates the liquid and milk solids from fat.

4. Alcohol and Vegetable Oils

Alcohol, beer, and spirits are all gluten products, which tend to be high in sugar and should thus be avoided. Likewise, avoid vegetable-based fats, as these could be inflammatory to body cells and therefore aren't recommended for you. Avoid:

- Beer

- Tequila

- Rum

- Vodka

- Alcohol and mixers

- Whiskey

- Sunflower oil

- Corn oil

- Safflower oil

With this information, you can quickly come up with all manner of delicious recipes and easy-to-follow meal plans. Before we get there, though, let's go back to the benefits you stand to derive by following the paleo diet.

CHAPTER 3

How To Start The Diet

A paleo diet is reported to free you from migraines, remove bloating, eliminate seasonal allergies, clear up your acne, and shed some pounds. While none of it's guaranteed, cleaning up the diet and focusing on fresh and whole foods is a good notion. Natural foods in appropriate portions help you feel reasonably satisfied as they aid in keeping the levels of blood sugar even and the hunger hormones quite balanced.

The main paleo for the starter's guidelines:

Skip all grains (both whole and refined), dairy, packaged snacks, legumes, and sugar in favor of veggies, fruits, meats, eggs, seafood, nuts, fats, seeds, and oils—sound easy, however, to go a cavewoman successfully takes savvy. You can follow these paleo diet principles, for starters.

Pinpoint Motivation

Most individuals turn to the paleo diet to assist with medical problems, like GI issues, allergies, and autoimmune conditions. Some have to feel good day-to-day or believe that it is a healthy way to have food. Your main reason would help you determine the guidelines you follow and what you need to be meticulous about. Also, be strict regarding your principles for the very first month. It's enough time to begin noticing good changes in your health.

Clean Out Kitchen

Collect all "no" food items on a paleo diet list such as packaged foods, grains, milk, cereal, cheese, vegetable oils, yogurt, and beans, you get this—and toss these in the dust bin. Doing this all has one advantage: it is easy to avoid the temptation when it is not there. But in case you like to take little steps at first, then it does work as well. Probably you can cut dairy items out during the first week, remove refined grains in the second week, and skip the grains during the third week, and so on until you are following the paleo diet. In each way, make sure to buy whole foods; hence you have got plenty to work with for designing the paleo diet meal plan.

Follow 85/15 Approach

After 1st 30 days, several experts suggest the 85/15 rule, which means 85% of the time you are strictly following the paleo diet, leaving 15% for the non-paleo, whether that is one granola bar (that you could opt for the paleo granola recipe), one hamburger (bun and all) at the cookout, or some cocktails. Focus on how you feel after introducing new things into the paleo diet. For instance, when you have one scoop of yummy ice cream and wake up bloating the following day, you might decide future discomfort is not worth this.

Cook

As the paleo diet is based on fresh and whole foods, it is easy to whip meals up at home than in a restaurant where it is hard to control what ingredients are there. So, take this golden opportunity to experiment with the new foods—it might be a bit challenging for you to purchase weird-looking veggies at the market and ask the shopkeeper for a piece of advice on how perfectly to cook it.

You could search online too or invest in the paleo diet cookbook for inspiration; hence the meals stay yummy and are not just plain chicken breast along with simple carrots and kale.

Expect 1 Setback (or 2)

It is normal to follow the paleo diet and slip back into the usual eating habits. But you need not worry about failure. It is a good learning process.

You can also search for like-minded people who are already following this diet via local forums, groups, blogs, and Facebook and connect with those to take assistance to keep you on track—and save you over there.

The Label Decoder

As you know to not eat doughnuts, crackers, and cookies, but a few foods are not paleo: nut jars of butter, peanut butter (this is a legume); dried fruit along with the added sugars; and lunchmeats, malt vinegar, soy sauce, and other sauces and marinades (some consist of sugar, soy, preservatives, and gluten). Hence make sure to see all ingredients list while purchasing anything in the package.

Think About Your Plate

You are taught to always reserve half a plate with vegetables, one quarter for the lean protein, and a remaining quarter for the whole grains. While you change to the paleo diet, stop holding someplace for the grains:

The balanced plate contains a palm-sized protein, one dollop of fats, and vegetables, vegetables, vegetables (fill the remaining container along with these).

Change Your Oil

Rather than reaching for the corn, canola, or soybean oil for frying, you will have to use lard or coconut oil. Really. Yes, these good-quality saturated fats are good to prepare food with as they are stable and will not oxidize while heated through (oxidation also releases harmful free radicals).

When this comes to the lard, animal fats—in case, from the grass-fed cows—were packed with vast amounts of omega 3 and one form of fat known as conjugated linoleic acid that some studies find might help you in burning fat.

Some dietitians also suggest butter from the grass-fed cows; however, many restrict dairy of all kinds. (The choice is all yours.) For cold applications, you can use walnut oil, olive oil, and avocado oil.

Eat Meat

Many people have restricted meat from the paleo diet as they believe that it is detrimental to health. You could also eat meat—only be sure that it is of high quality. Hence, you can say bye to the processed meats that include bologna, hot dogs, and salami.

Wild meats such as bison, boar, and elk are an excellent choice for you, followed by pasture-fed poultry as well as meats, and lean grain-fed meat must be the last pick. And, for seafood, go for the wild-caught quite often, and low-mercury and sustainable choices are the best.

You can Easily Make Fool Your Sweet Tooth.

Removing sugar is one primary arduous task for several people at the start. In case you love to eat a treat right after your dinner, then you can swap your cookies or just for you for one piece of the fruit. (For your sugar cravings, experts say that the paleo diet allows dried mangoes.)

With time, the taste buds would adjust accordingly—and that the Oreos that you loved a lot before may become so much sweet for you now. Seriously, it can happen!

You can Eat Out

Some business dinner and brunch with the best friends is possible on a paleo diet. All that takes is just a bit of ingredient sleuthing. You need to first look at your menu before time and pick 1 to 2 options you could paleo-size.

This can be wild salmon and broccoli. (Also request double the vegetables rather than the rice pilaf.) Also, at a restaurant, do not be ashamed to ask relevant questions regarding the things that are prepared and request alterations, if necessary.

Eat the Whole Foods which are Nutrient Rich

In case food isn't in such a state that this was while pulled from the soil, then there are great chances that it has been refined and is not optimal. By selecting food right from nature, our bodies give our bodies those nutrients required to heal our bodies.

Avoid Nutrient-Poor, Processed, and Refined Foods which are Made in the Factory

It means that the pasteurized dairy, grains, seed oils (canola, cottonseed, corn, and soybean), artificial sweeteners, and refined sugar (fructose corn syrup). Most of these food items rob nutrients from the body for digestion that negates the primary aim of eating that must fuel a human body and nutrients for growing and repairing itself.

Yeah, it would take some time to learn about the paleo lifestyle. There might be some confusion at the start while working to change the grocery shopping habits, eating outside, and meal preparation; hence, this is vital to alter at a gradual pace that suits you perfectly. Plus, know that the most "non-paleo" foods have to be re-worked to fit the paleo lifestyle.

Eat For Healthy Digestive System

Gut/brain health is of utmost importance for overall health. For being successful, you have to focus on the signs that the body is giving you. In case you come to know that consuming dairy causes some digestive upset, then it's the way your body of telling you about avoiding such food items! Keeping your food log and journal could help you spot the latest food consumption trends and signs. Digestive health is more crucial than many people think. Do you know 60 to 80 percent of the immune system begins in the gut? In case you are continuously stressing digestion with some irritating foods, then the immune system would be suppressed, and your health would suffer a lot.

Eat Food to Keep Steady Blood Sugar

Have you ever felt weak or shaky between your meals? Do you have some swings in the energy level? Chances are, the blood sugar is spiking and dropping due to the meals. If you eat sugar and white flour, then the blood sugar will spike up, and you will feel the rush of energy. While the sugar is managed automatically by the body, your blood sugar also drops, and you start to feel hungry and lethargic. Consuming whole foods would give the body carbs, enough proteins, and an ample amount of fats. The combination would let your blood sugar rise even more slowly after having meals and staying elevated between your meals.

As the paleo diet is all about consuming whole foods so it might be good for everybody. The main thing is that this could be easily customized to fit anybody. Keeping one journal about how do you feel throughout the day might make the whole process work smoothly.

CHAPTER 4

How To Maintain The Diet

Paleo is truly trouble-free if you mostly stay at your house, but what about when you go outside? If you love to go outside from time to time, your Paleo lifestyle might be compromised because you will have no access to Paleo-friendly cooking equipment and ingredients. That's why your weight loss progress might slow down.

But do not tremble because you can still consume Paleo while you are outside. Here are some ways on how to do it!

Be Ready

A crucial factor while attempting to stay Paleo while outside is to be ready at all times. Envision yourself for accomplishment from the start and sketch for your prototype of what will happen in the future. Determine when your primary shortcomings will occur so that you can be ready if you come across them.

Just focus on your diet and do not mind what other people will tell you since many of them are not acquainted with what Paleo is all about. They might think that you are crazy, but you know that you are just trying to be healthy, which is the most important.

Target At Least 80 Percent

If you are on the road, always reduce some slack. It is assumed that it will not be completely perfect this time. Furthermore, if you are on Paleo, being outside is difficult, so do not lose hope if you fail when you first try eating Paleo while outdoors. Target to consume Paleo-friendly foods 80% and scale it up as time goes by. A skipped meal or a below-average snack selection here and there won't inflict significant damage to you but be sure that you do not overdo it.

Instead of attempting to be entirely under Paleo while engaging in gatherings, which is super challenging to do, target at least 80 percent.

The foods that are mostly served there are not aligned with the Paleo diet, so that is why you must lower your expectations so that you will not become frustrated at the end which. We can conclude that 80 percent is the best threshold for your Paleo percentage while outdoors.

Be Intelligent Enough When Eating on a Restaurant

If you are going for a lunch out, it's undoubtedly the best way to select your strategy depends on the kind of restaurants you will enter. The most extraordinary suggestion is to keep out from the sides or interchange them out for fruits or veggies.

Mexican

Mexican food is perfect for Paleo dieters if you can keep out from chips and the tacos. The most advisable Paleo Mexican food right now is fajitas because you can consume the veggies and meat from the container and leave the tortillas behind or give it to other people.

Sushi

Sushi is a great selection too. While rice isn't entirely paleo, some foods are much inferior to it.

Keep in mind that lots of sushi rice have tremendous amounts of sugar, so don't ever overeat, but it is tolerable in small quantities. Just concentrate on the seafood, not on the rice. That is the best thing that you can do.

Steakhouses

If you are engaging with your customers, it is advisable to go to a steakhouse. Not only will you electrify your customers, but you will also consume delicious foods. There is a high percentage that you can find a lot of Paleo foods in steakhouses.

Just do not mind the sides, only target the main course, and you'll possess more than sufficient to satisfy your hunger.

American

You will be satisfied at these restaurants if you keep out from chips, fries, and buns. These restaurants usually produce higher quality meat sources than other places. They typically have amazing veggies as sides, and you can typically consume an excellent burger and fruits and veggies as a side dish.

Italian

Always keep out from Italian cuisine. If that's not a resort, only consume the meatballs or chicken and Caesar salad. No pasta and other stuff, and it will be worth it.

Appetizers and Sides

You can wholly replace fries for a Caesar salad, and you must seize this opportunity if you have the privilege of having one.

Water Intake

When you are on Paleo, you must ensure that you are taking a sufficient amount of water. As you are more exposed to meats, it is suggested that you will pair them with proper consumption of water. In this way, you can balance out your fluids in the body and at the same time promote good digestion.

It is suitable for both our kidneys and colon. That is why it is recommended to take at least 2 - 3 liters of water daily. So if you always go outdoors, do not forget to bring your water jug from time to time to cope with your daily water requirements.

Outdoor Foods Suggestions

If you know that you will be on a road trip, always prepare your Paleo foods, and remove all the worries you have regarding your diet.

- Snacks

- Nuts

- Beef Jerky

- Dark chocolate must have 80 percent and above cacao content

- Fruits

- Apples

- Oranges

- Berries

If you prefer foods that are easy to swallow, inspect the dried fruits in the market. They are tasty and trouble-free to consume and are not messy. However, be mindful of the tremendous amount of fructose before you decide to destroy them.

Veggies

They are typically considered "go-to" snacks. Just clean them, and they usually are prepared to consume them. You can likely consume them while you are traveling, which makes it very advantageous for you. Here the suggested list of the veggies that you can consume.

- Avocado

- Spinach

- Carrots

- Raw broccoli

- Celery

Purchase from the Market or Grocery

Being well-versed in the products you can buy in grocery stores or the market is beneficial in your Paleo diet. It significantly enhances your capacity to consume Paleo while you are outdoors.

While it can be rugged to ready a meal if you don't possess complete equipment in your place, you might be able to look for some fresh or prepared food at a nearby market. Some markets cut the meat for you so that you will cook it afterward.

If you have your car, you can bring a container to pile up your food. The box will let you possess compact and fresh foods, which will be beneficial while you are on a strict Paleo diet. You can also have an entire chicken or a semi-cooked chicken and eat that, or you can drop by at the lunch section on the market and take your meal there.

CHAPTER 5

Breakfast

1. Avocado Burger With Salmon

Preparation time: 10 minutes
Cooking Time: 20 minutes
Servings: 1
Ingredients:
- 1 Avocado
- 2 Slices Of Smoked Salmon
- Sesame Seeds

Directions:
1. Cut the avocado in half.
2. Peel it.
3. Remove the core.
4. Place the smoked salmon in between the two an avocado part.
5. Add some sesame seeds.

Nutrition:
Calories 60
Fat 2.3
Fiber 0.8
Carbs 5
Protein 5.6

2. Banana Mango Smoothie

Preparation time: 5 minutes
Cooking Time: 10 minutes
Servings: 1
Ingredients:
- 1 Banana
- 1 Mango
- 1 Cup Of Coconut Milk

Directions:
1. Peel the banana and slice it.
2. Peel the mango and cut it.
3. Use a mixer to whisk the fruits and milk together, keep some pieces of fruits for decoration.
4. Serve the smoothie in a glass and decorate it.

Nutrition:
Calories: 32 Fat: 5
Fiber: 2
Carbs: 11
Protein: 4

3. American Breakfast

Preparation time: 2 minutes
Cooking time: 5 minutes Servings: 1
Ingredients:

- 2 Eggs
- 1/2 Cup Almond Milk
- 6 Slices Of Bacon
- Vegetable Oil

Directions:

1. Set the eggs in a bowl and whisk.
2. Add the milk
3. Preheat 2 pans over medium heat.
4. In one pan cook the bacon for about 5 minutes
5. In the other pan add some vegetable oil and scramble the eggs.

Nutrition:
Calories: 13 Fat: 4 Fiber: 5
Carbs: 23 Protein: 8

4. Chocolate Brownies

Preparation time: 10 minutes
Cooking time: 25 minutes Servings: 3
Ingredients:

- 4 Eggs
- 1/2 Cup Cocoa Powder
- 2 Cups Of Almonds Okra
- 6 Tbsp. Of Honey
- 1 Tsp. Of Vanilla Powder
- Salt
- 1 Tsp. Of Baking Soda
- Coconut Oil

Directions:

1. In a bowl set the eggs and beat them with the honey.
2. Add the warm coconut oil and mix.
3. In another bowl mix the okra with the cocoa powder, the vanilla powder, the salt and baking soda.
4. Mix the two bowls ingredients together.
5. Pour the ingredients in a baking tin and cook in the oven for 25 minutes (340 F).

Nutrition:
Calories: 32 Fat: 5 Fiber: 2 Carbs: 11 Protein: 4

5. Almond Milk Homemade

Preparation time: 10 minutes   Cooking Time: 15 minutes Servings: 1 bottle of almond milk
Ingredients

- 2 Cups Of Shelled Organic Almonds
- A Pinch Of Salt
- 4 Cups Of Still Water
- 1 Filter Bag FOR VEGETABLE MILK

Directions:

1. Put 4 cups of still water in a glass container, dip the almonds in the water and add a pinch of salt.
2. Let the almonds dip in the water for 12 hours. Then rinse the almonds with clean water.
3. Put the almonds in the mixer. Add 2 cups of still water. Set the mixer and let it work for 1-2 minutes or until a well-mixed compound is obtained.
4. Filter the mixture obtained through a filter bag for vegetable milk. Place the bag on a container, pour the almond mixture into the bag and squeeze with your hands to filter the liquid.
5. Set the almond milk into a glass container with a hermetic lid and refrigerate for 3 days.
6. Shake the container before use since the liquid separates.

Nutrition:
Calories: 13 Fat: 9 Fiber: 12 Carbs: 21 Protein: 8

6. Eggs Benedict With Hollandaise Sauce

Preparation time: 15 minutes
Cooking time: 20 minutes Servings: 2
Ingredients:

- 2 potato toasts
- 2 eggs
- 2 bacon slices
- Apple vinegar
- Salt
- Green onion
- Coconut oil
- 1 cup of water
- 2 yolks
- 1 Tbsp. of lemon juice
- Salt
- Pepper
- 1/2 cup of ghee

Directions:

1. Mix the yolks, the water and the lemon juice together in a bowl. Set the bowl in a pan filled with some boiling water.
2. Place the pan on the heat and beat the yolks until you obtain a thick and frothy compound. Add salt pepper and the ghee and keep on beating for about 5 minutes.
3. Cook the bacon and prepare the poached eggs.
4. Serve the dish placing the potato toast with one bacon slice and the egg on top of it. Add 2 spoons of sauce.

Nutrition:
Calories: 23 Fat: 11 Fiber: 12 Carbs: 25 Protein: 9

7. Shitake Mushrooms And Seaweed Omelets

Preparation time: 10 minutes
Cooking time: 15 minutes
Servings: 2
Ingredients:

- 3 Eggs
- 1/2 Cup Of Shitake Mushrooms
- 1 Tsp. 0f Seaweed Flakes
- Salt
- 1 Tbsp. Of Coconut OIL

Directions:

1. Rinse the mushrooms and cut them into pieces.
2. Beat the eggs in a bowl with seaweed flakes and salt.
3. Warmth the coconut oil in a pan and add the mushrooms, cook for 5 minutes. Season with some salt.
4. Pour the eggs in the pan and cook for 10 minutes.

Nutrition:
Calories: 21
Fat: 4
Fiber: 2
Carbs: 15
Protein: 5

8. Crunchy Green Bananas Sticks

Preparation time: 5 minutes
Cooking time: 10 minutes
Servings: 2
Ingredients:

- 2 Green bananas
- 3 Tbsp. of nuts
- 3 Tbsp. of almonds
- 1 Tbsp. of coconut sugar
- 1/2 tsp. of cinnamon
- 2 Tbsp. of coconut oil

Directions:

1. Mix the nuts and the almonds in a mixer. In a bowl, mix the compound together with the coconut sugar and cinnamon.
2. Peel and cut the bananas into strips.
3. Dip the strips into the nuts and almonds mixture.
4. Preheat a pan over medium heat with some coconut oil; cook 3-4 strips by time until golden.

Nutrition:
Calories: 13 Fat: 8
Fiber: 12
Carbs: 21
Protein: 5

9. Chinese Steamed Eggs

Preparation time: 5 minutes
Cooking time: 15 minutes
Servings: 2
Ingredients:

- 2 eggs
- 1 cup of water
- Salt
- 1 Tbsp. of minced green onion
- 1 tsp. of sesame seeds

Directions:
1. Beat the eggs with a fork, add water and salt.
2. Filter the compound into two heat resistant bowls.
3. Boil some water into a pan, when the water starts boiling put the bowl into a bamboo basket and place the basket on the pan.
4. Cover the bowls with some baking paper and the lid. Cook for 15 minutes
5. Roast the sesame seeds in a pan.
6. Season the eggs with the seeds and some minced green onion.

Nutrition:
Calories: 13 Fat: 8
Fiber: 12 Carbs: 21 Protein: 5

10. Matcha Mint Iced Tea

Preparation time: 5 minutes
Cooking Time: 5 minutes Servings: 3
Ingredients:

- 4 Tbsp. of green Matcha tea ceremonial grade
- 1 lemon fresh juice
- 4 fresh mint twigs
- 4 cups of water

Directions:
1. Put the green tea in a glass, add a little bit of water and mix with milk frothier or a chosen.
2. Pour the tea in an airtight jar and add the lemon juice and the fresh mint. Add the remaining water and stir.
3. Let it rest until cold.

Nutrition:
Calories: 32
Fat: 5
Fiber: 2
Carbs: 11
Protein: 4

11. Coconut Truffles

Preparation time: 1 hour
Cooking Time: 20 minutes
Servings: 14 truffles
Ingredients:

- 1 cup of grated coconut
- 4 Tbsp. of almonds
- 4 Tbsp. of cashews
- 4 Tbsp. of walnuts
- 1 Tbsp. of honey
- 1/4 tsp. of vanilla powder
- 1 Tbsp. of coconut milk
- 3 Tbsp. of coconut oil
- 14 almonds

- Grated coconut for decoration

Directions:
1. In a mixer mix the almonds, the cashews, the walnuts and the grated coconut. (Keep 14 almonds for the filling).
2. Add the coconut oil, the honey, the vanilla powder and the coconut milk and mix again.
3. Shape 15 grams balls, and fill each of them with 1 almond.
4. Roll them into the grated coconut and refrigerate for 1 hour.

Nutrition:
Calories: 13
Fat: 15
Fiber: 6
Carbs: 15
Protein: 3

12. Soft Strawberry Cake

Preparation time: 15 minutes
Cooking time: 45 minutes
Servings: 6
Ingredients:
- 1 cup of almonds flour
- 1/3 cup of arrowroot
- 4 eggs
- 1/2 lb. of strawberries
- 3 Tbsp. of honey
- 1/4 tsp. of vanilla powder
- 1 tsp. of baking soda
- Salt
- 5 Tbsp. of ghee

Directions:
1. Beat the eggs together with the honey, add the heated ghee.
2. In another bowl mix almond flour, vanilla powder, baking soda, arrowroot and salt.
3. Mix the two compounds together.
4. Cut the strawberries into 4 pieces.
5. Pour the compound in a baking tin covered with some baking paper, add the strawberries.
6. Cook in the oven for 45 minutes (330F).

Nutrition:
Calories: 43 Fat: 17
Fiber: 8 Carbs: 21 Protein: 7

13. Chestnuts And Walnuts Cookies

Preparation time: 10 minutes
Cooking time: 20 minutes
Servings: 13 cookies
Ingredients:
- 1 cup of chestnuts flour
- 1/2 cup of walnuts flour
- 1 egg
- 3 Tbsp. of coconut sugar
- 1/2 tsp. of baking soda
- 3 Tbsp. of ghee
- 13 walnuts (for decoration)

Directions:
1. Mix the dry ingredients in a bowl.
2. In another bowl mix the egg with the heated ghee.
3. Mix the two bowls compound together.
4. Shape 13 balls and put them in baking tin covered with baking paper.
5. Place one walnut on top of every ball and cook in the oven for 20 minutes (330F).

Nutrition:
Calories: 13 Fat: 21 Fiber: 14 Carbs: 32 Protein: 9

14. Avocado, Chocolate And Orange Mousse

Preparation time: 75 minutes

Cooking Time: 20 minutes

Servings: 3

Ingredients:

- 1 avocado
- 3 Tbsp. of cocoa powder
- 1 orange
- 1 Tbsp. of honey

Directions:

1. Cut in half the orange. Squeeze one half and cut in pieces the other one.
2. In a mixer mix the avocado pulp, cocoa powder, honey, 3 Tbsp. of orange juice.
3. Place the mixture in some cups and set in the fridge for 1 hour.
4. Decorate with the orange's pieces.

Nutrition:

Calories: 32

Fat: 5

Fiber: 2

Carbs: 11

Protein: 4

15. Spinach Crepes

Preparation time: 10 minutes

Cooking time: 10 minutes

Servings: 6 crepes

Ingredients:

- 1/4 lb. of spinach
- 3 eggs
- 2 Tbsp. of coconut flour
- 1 Tbsp. of arrowroot flour
- 1/3 cup of coconut milk
- 1/4 cup of water
- Salt
- Coconut oil

Directions:

1. Mix all the ingredients out of the coconut oil in a mixer-.
2. Grease a pan with some coconut oil; put 3 tbsp. of the compound. Cook for 1 minute then turn the crepe.
3. Repeat with the remaining mixture.

Nutrition:

Calories: 31 Fat: 12

Fiber: 7 Carbs: 21 Protein: 8

16. Scrambled Eggs With Lox

Preparation time: 5 minutes

Cooking time: 15 minutes

Servings: 1

Ingredients:

- 1 tablespoon olive or coconut oil
- 1/2 small red onion, diced
- 3 large eggs
- 2 ounces smoked salmon, chopped
- Freshly ground black pepper, to taste
- 1 large tomato, sliced
- 1 teaspoon capers
- 1 tablespoon fresh parsley, chopped

Directions

1. Warmth oil in a medium skillet and add the onions. Cook until soft.
2. Beat the eggs in a small bowl and add the salmon. Season with freshly ground black pepper. Pour egg mixture over onions and scramble until cooked through.
3. To serve, top the tomato slices with the eggs and garnish with capers and parsley.

Nutrition:

Calories: 32

Fat: 5

Fiber: 2

Carbs: 11

Protein: 4

17. Chicken With Sweet Potato Hash Browns

Preparation time: 15 minutes
Cooking time: 15 minutes
Servings: 4
Ingredients:

- 2 sweet potatoes, strip and diced into small pieces
- 2 tablespoons olive oil
- 1/2 small onion, diced
- 4 chicken thighs, cooked, meat pulled off bones and chopped or shredded
- 1 teaspoon each, dried thyme and oregano
- Freshly ground black pepper, to taste

Directions:

1. Steam sweet potatoes until juicy and easily pierced with a fork. Slice in half and puree one half with a fork or potato masher.
2. In a large skillet, warmth oil over medium-high heat. Attach onion and cook until tender. Attach chicken and spices, except pepper, and merge.
3. Attach both sweet potato mixtures to the pan and merge the mixture thoroughly. Flavor with freshly ground black pepper.
4. Cook until browned on the bottom. Break up into small pieces and serve.

Nutrition:
Calories: 21 Fat: 4 Fiber: 1 Carbs: 21 Protein: 6

18. Paleo Muffins

Preparation time: 15 minutes
Cooking time: 15 minutes Servings: 12
Ingredients:

- 1 teaspoon olive or coconut oil
- 1/2 medium onion, chopped
- 1 cup broccoli, finely chopped
- 1/2 green bell pepper, diced
- 1/2 red bell pepper, diced
- 8 large eggs
- Freshly ground black pepper, to taste

Directions:

1. Set oven to 400 degrees F. Brush a muffin tin with oil. Mix veggies in a large bowl and divide equally among muffin tins.
2. Beat eggs in a large bowl. Season with freshly ground black pepper. Pour mixture over veggies in the muffin pan.
3. Bake until tops are browned. Cool before serving.

Nutrition:
Calories: 21
Fat: 9
Fiber: 14
Carbs: 21
Protein: 7

19. Paleo Huevos Rancheros

Preparation time: 10 minutes
Cooking time: 20 minutes
Servings: 1
Ingredients:

- 1 tablespoon olive or coconut oil
- 2 cloves garlic, minced
- 1 red bell pepper, chopped
- 1/2 small onion, diced
- 1 jalapeño pepper, minced
- 2 large eggs
- Freshly ground black pepper, to taste
- 1/2 cup prepared salsa
- 1/2 medium avocado, sliced

Directions:

1. Set oil in a medium skillet over medium heat. Add the garlic, bell pepper, onion, and jalapeño pepper, and sauté until soft. Attach the eggs and cook until the whites are cooked through. Season with freshly ground black pepper.
2. To serve, top the eggs and veggies with salsa and avocado. Serve immediately.

Nutrition:
Calories: 32
Fat: 7

Fiber: 3
Carbs: 27
Protein: 4

20. Classic French Omelet

Preparation time: 10 minutes
Cooking time: 20 minutes
Servings: 1
Ingredients:

- 3 large eggs
- 1 tablespoon olive or coconut oil
- 2 tablespoons chopped fresh herbs of your option
- Freshly ground black pepper, to taste
- 2 slices minimally processed ham

Directions:

1. Whisk eggs and set aside. Warmth a non-stick skillet over medium heat and add the oil.
2. Add eggs, followed by herbs. Season with freshly ground black pepper. Cook for 1 minute and add the ham to the center. When the eggs begin to cook, fold both sides toward the center.
3. Set onto a plate and serve with extra ham slices and herbs for garnish.

Nutrition:
Calories: 12
Fat: 4
Fiber: 3
Carbs: 13
Protein: 5

21. Homemade Breakfast Patties

Preparation time: 10 minutes
Cooking time: 15 minutes
Servings: 4
Ingredients:

- 1 pound ground pork
- 1 teaspoon garlic powder
- 1 teaspoon paprika
- 1/2 teaspoon ground sage
- 1 teaspoon fennel seeded
- 1/4 teaspoon cayenne pepper
- 1/4 teaspoon white pepper
- 2 tablespoons olive or coconut oil
- Freshly ground black pepper, to taste

Directions:

1. Using your hands, combine the pork with the seasonings in a large bowl until well combined.
2. Form into 8 to 10 patties. Warmth a medium skillet over medium heat and add the oil. Fry the sausage patties until golden brown on both sides (about 4 minutes per side); making sure the inside is no longer pink. Season with freshly ground black pepper.
3. Serve immediately.

Nutrition:
Calories: 13
Fat: 21
Fiber: 14
Carbs: 32
Protein: 9

22. Paleo Western Omelet

Preparation time: 10 minutes
Cooking time: 15 minutes
Servings: 1
Ingredients:

- 3 large eggs
- 1 tablespoon olive oil
- 2 ounces minimally processed, thick-cut ham
- 1/4 cup chopped bell pepper
- 1/4 cup onion, chopped
- 1/2 cup spinach, finely chopped
- Freshly ground black pepper, to taste

Directions

1. Beat the eggs until frothy.
2. Add oil to a non-stick omelet pan and heat over medium heat.
3. Add eggs. As they start to set, add the ham and veggies, spreading evenly throughout.
4. Fold over and finish cooking. Season with freshly ground black pepper. When eggs are thoroughly cooked, slide onto a plate and serve.

Nutrition:
Calories: 13
Fat: 4
Fiber: 5
Carbs: 23
Protein: 8

23. Caveman French Toast

Preparation time: 10 minutes
Cooking time: 15 minutes
Servings: 2
Ingredients:

- 4 large eggs
- 1 tablespoon water
- 1 teaspoon vanilla extract
- 1 teaspoon cinnamon
- Pinch of nutmeg
- 1 tablespoon coconut oil
- Pure maple syrup for drizzling

Directions
1. In a small bowl, set the eggs and water together until frothy. Add vanilla, cinnamon, and nutmeg.
2. Heat a non-stick omelet pan on medium-high heat. When hot, add coconut oil and swirl pan to coat.
3. Add half the egg mixture to the pan and let it cook through before flipping. Cook until browned on both sides.

Nutrition:
Calories: 21
Fat: 9
Fiber: 14
Carbs: 21
Protein: 7

24. Italian Frittata

Preparation time: 10 minutes
Cooking time: 0 minutes Servings: 6
Ingredients:

- 2 tablespoons olive oil
- 1 small onion, diced
- 2 cloves garlic, minced
- 1 zucchini, diced
- 1 pound spinach, coarsely chopped
- 12 cherry tomatoes, quartered
- 1/2 cup black olives
- Freshly ground black pepper, to taste
- 12 large eggs

Directions:
1. Preheat oven to 375 degrees F.
2. In a large sauté pan, set the oil over medium-high heat. Add the onions and garlic and cook until soft. Attach the zucchini and continue cooking for a couple more minutes. Add spinach, combine and cook until wilted. Detach pan from heat and add the tomatoes and olives. Season with freshly ground black pepper.
3. In a large bowl, set the eggs until frothy.
4. Lightly brush the bottom of an 8 x 13-inch casserole dish with oil. Add the veggies to the dish. Set over the egg mixture and stir to combine.
5. Bake for an hour until the top is browned and the center is cooked through. Slice into squares and serve.

Nutrition:
Calories: 21
Fat: 5
Fiber: 3
Carbs: 21
Protein: 7

25. Paleo Granola

Preparation time: 10 minutes
Cooking time: 20 minutes Servings: 8
Ingredients:

- 1 cup raw pecans
- 1 cup raw sunflower seeds
- 1 cup raw walnuts
- 1 cup raw sliced almonds
- 1 cup raw pumpkin seeds
- 1 cup unsweetened coconut, shredded
- 1 cup Medjool dates, chopped
- 1 cup raisins

Directions:

1. Dip nuts and seeds overnight in warm water, about 10 hours. Drain well.
2. Scatter the nuts and seeds on a baking sheet. Heat oven to the lowest temperature possible and place the baking sheet in the oven door open dehydrate nuts for 10 hours. Allow to cool completely.
3. Slice nuts and seeds and merge with the coconut, dates, and raisins. Serve.

Nutrition:
Calories: 12 Fat: 11
Fiber: 9 Carbs: 25
Protein: 4

26. Paleo Waffles

Preparation time: 10 minutes
Cooking time: 20 minutes Servings: 2
Ingredients:

- 1/4 cup coconut flour
- 4 large eggs
- 1 tablespoon coconut milk
- 1 tablespoon cinnamon
- 1/4 teaspoon nutmeg
- 1/4 teaspoon baking soda
- Pure maple syrup

Directions:

1. Preheat a waffle iron. Merge all ingredients in a blender or by hand in a bowl. Pour batter in the center of the waffle iron, covering the entire surface area.
2. Cook until waffles release from the iron. Serve immediately with maple syrup.

Nutrition:
Calories: 12
Fat: 4
Fiber: 3
Carbs: 13
Protein: 5

27. Paleo Spinach Quiche

Preparation time: 10 minutes
Cooking time: 15 minutes Servings: 4-6
Ingredients:

- 1 teaspoon olive oil, plus more for garnish
- 1 cup chopped fresh spinach
- 1/2 cup chopped red onion
- 1/2 teaspoon salt
- 1/2 teaspoon freshly ground black pepper
- 1/2 teaspoon ground nutmeg
- 8 large eggs, beaten
- 1/2 cup plain almond milk

Directions:

1. Set oven to 350 F. Grease a 9-inch glass pie plate.
2. In a small skillet, set the olive oil over medium heat, and sauté the spinach, onion, salt, pepper, and nutmeg for about 5 minutes or just until the onions are translucent.
3. Stir the eggs and almond milk together in a small bowl. Add the spinach mixture, stir, and pour into the pie plate.
4. Bake the quiche on the middle oven rack for 30 to 40 minutes, or until the center is completely set. Serve warm or at room temperature.

Nutrition:
Calories: 13 Fat: 4 Fiber: 5 Carbs: 23 Protein: 8

28. Banana-Berry Pancakes

Preparation time: 10 minutes
Cooking time: 15 minutes
Servings: 2
Ingredients:

- 6 egg whites, lightly beaten
- 2 bananas, mashed
- 1/3 cup raspberries, mashed
- 2 tablespoons almond butter
- 1/4 teaspoon cinnamon

Directions:

1. Set a skillet or griddle with cooking spray. In a large bowl, merge the egg whites, bananas, raspberries, and almond butter until smooth.
2. Pour the butter into the skillet using 1/2 cup for each pancake. Flip the pancakes Serve with a sprinkling of cinnamon and/or fresh fruit.

Nutrition:
Calories: 15
Fat: 5
Fiber: 13
Carbs: 23
Protein: 3

29. High Fiber Bacon And Eggs

Preparation time: 10 minutes
Cooking time: 15 minutes
Servings: 2
Ingredients:

- 6 slices of uncured, nitrate-free, thick-cut bacon
- 1 tablespoon olive or coconut oil
- 2 cups cabbage, shredded
- Freshly ground black pepper, to taste
- 4 large eggs

Directions:

1. Lay bacon on a sheet pan and preheat the broiler to high. Put bacon under the broiler and broil for 5 to 6 minutes per side, until desired crispness.
2. Warmth the oil in a skillet and add the cabbage. Cook until soft, browned, and lightly crisp. Season with pepper. Remove from pan and place on two plates.
3. Crack the eggs in the pan and cook until desired doneness. Season with freshly ground black pepper. To set, place the eggs on top of the cabbage and serve with the broiled bacon.

Nutrition:
Calories: 12
Fat: 4
Fiber: 3
Carbs: 13

Protein: 5

30. Eggplant Holes

Preparation time: 10 minutes
Cooking time: 15 minutes Servings: 2
Ingredients:

- 1 medium eggplant
- 2 tablespoons olive or coconut oil
- 4 large eggs
- Green onions, chopped, for garnish
- Freshly ground black pepper, to taste

Directions:

1. Slice eggplant into 1-inch thick slices and season with pepper. Using a small cookie cutter, cut a hole in the center of each slice.
2. Heat a large skillet over medium-high heat. Add the oil, followed by the eggplant. Beat one egg into the center of each slice. Cook for 2 to 3 minutes and then flip, being careful not to let the egg fall out of the hole. Cook for another 2 minutes and detach from pan. Season with freshly ground black pepper. Garnish with the green onions and serve.

Nutrition:
Calories: 32 Fat: 5
Fiber: 2
Carbs: 11-Protein: 4

CHAPTER 6

Lunch

31. Pan-Fried Vegetables With Green And White Asparagus

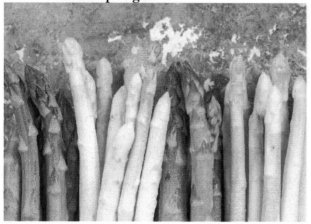

Preparation time: 10 minutes
Cooking time: 15 minutes Servings: 4
Ingredients:

- 400 g green asparagus
- 400 g white asparagus
- 300 g tofu
- 300 g cherry tomatoes
- 1 onion
- 1 clove of garlic
- 2 tbsp. olive oil
- 4 tbsp. water
- 1 tbsp. sesame seeds
- salt and pepper

Directions:
1. Remove the skin from the white asparagus, cut off the ends, cut into small pieces and cook in boiling salted and sugar water for about five minutes. Rinse the asparagus and set aside. Wash the green asparagus and cut off the ends and cut into small pieces.
2. Clean the cherry tomatoes and cut them in half. Detach the peel from the onion and the clove of garlic and dice. Cut the tofu into cubes. Sear the tofu in the olive oil for about five minutes. It should get a little crispy.

Steam the onion in the pan. Then add the green asparagus and fry for about five minutes. Mix in the garlic and fry in the pan for five minutes.
3. Add the cherry tomatoes and white asparagus and stir in. Let everything simmer with the water for about two minutes. Season with a little salt and pepper to taste and garnish with the sesame seeds.

Nutrition:
Calories: 21 Fat: 9 Fiber: 2 Carbs: 21 Protein: 9

32. Spinach And Tomato Frittata

Preparation time: 10 minutes Cooking time: 15 minutes Servings: 6
Ingredients:

- 12 eggs
- 500 g cherry tomatoes
- 200 g spinach, frozen
- 2 onions
- 200 g ricotta
- 2 handfuls of basil
- 2 tbsp. olive oil
- salt and pepper

Directions:
1. Thaw the frozen spinach and drain the liquid.
2. Set the oven to a temperature of 200 C with a fan. Grease the baking dish with butter.
3. Whisk the eggs and mix with a whisk. Season with a little salt and pepper. Pick the basil.
4. Remove the skin from the onions, divide in the middle and cut into fine slices. Set the tomatoes and cut them in half.
5. Bring a pan with oil to temperature and fry the onions on high temperature for four minutes. Then add the tomatoes and sweat for a minute.
6. Turn the heat down and add the spinach. Steam for three minutes. Then add the basil to the pan and mix until it collapses.

7. Put the vegetables in the baking dish and spread the ricotta on top.
8. Spread the egg mixture over the vegetables and bake the frittata in the oven for about half an hour. Serve with fresh basil and tomato halves.

Nutrition:
Calories: 43 Fat: 11 Fiber: 8 Carbs: 21 Protein: 5

33. Mozzarella Omelet With Grilled Tomatoes

Preparation time: 10 minutes Cooking time: 20 minutes Servings: 2
Ingredients:
For the grilled tomatoes

- 3 medium-sized tomatoes
- 1 teaspoon olive oil - salt and pepper
- 3 tbsp. grated parmesan
- 0.5 tsp. herbs of Provence
- Olive oil, for the baking dish

For the omelet

- 0.5 scoops of reduced-fat mozzarella, 8.5% fat
- 4 black olives - 3 sun-dried tomatoes
- 4 eggs - 4 tbsp. milk, 1.5% fat
- 0.25 teaspoon sweet paprika powder
- salt and pepper
- 2 teaspoons of olive oil - 4 basil leaves

Directions:
1. For the grilled tomatoes, preheat the grill to a temperature of 200 C. Clean the tomatoes, detach the stems and cut the tomatoes in half crosswise. Brush a sufficiently large baking dish with olive oil, put the tomatoes in with the cut surface facing up, and drizzle with olive oil and season with salt. Mix the parmesan with the herbs and a little pepper and sprinkle on the tomatoes. Grill these in the oven on medium heat for about ten minutes.
2. For the omelet, dry the mozzarella. Remove the core from the olives and cut into slices. Dice the dried tomatoes and the mozzarella. Merge the eggs with the milk in a bowl and season the egg milk with the paprika powder, salt and pepper. Mix the mozzarella, olives and sun-dried tomatoes into the egg mixture.
3. Bring the oil to temperature in a non-stick pan, pour in the egg mixture and let it set over medium heat for three minutes until the underside is brown. Turn and fry on the second side as well. Halve the omelet, cover with the basil leaves and serve with the grilled tomatoes.

Nutrition:
Calories: 32 Fat: 5 Fiber: 2 Carbs: 11 Protein: 4

34. Frittata Topping With Vegetables

Preparation time: 10 minutes
Cooking time: 20 minutes
Servings: 4
Ingredients:
For the frittata

- 100 g silken tofu
- 1 tbsp. cornstarch
- 1 tbsp. soy flour
- 1 tbsp. yeast flakes
- 0.5 tsp. kala namak
- 0.5 tsp. turmeric powder
- 0.5 tsp. curry powder
- 0.5 tsp. freshly grated nutmeg
- salt and pepper
- 60 g natural soy yoghurt

For the vegetables

- 200 g zucchini
- 100 g mushrooms
- 1 small, red pepper
- 1 onion
- 1 clove of garlic
- 1 tbsp. neutral oil
- salt and pepper

Directions:
1. Drain the silken tofu for the topping. Put the soy yoghurt, the cornstarch, the soy flour and the yeast flakes in a mixing bowl and puree everything with a hand blender until

creamy. Season the mixture with the turmeric, curry powder, nutmeg and kala namak, salt and pepper.
2. For the vegetables, clean, wash and dice the zucchini. Clean the mushrooms rub with kitchen paper and cut into slices. Cut the pepper in halves; remove the seeds, wash and dice. Remove the onion and garlic from the skin and chop.
3. Set the oven to 175 C. Heat the oil in a large pan and sauté the onions with the garlic until translucent. Fry the mushrooms, zucchini and bell pepper cubes over medium heat for about five minutes while stirring. Season with salt and pepper. Then take it off the stove.
4. Spread the icing on the vegetables. Bake the frittata in the stove (on the middle rack, fan oven at a temperature of 160) for half an hour until golden yellow. Let rest for 10 minutes before cutting.

Nutrition:
Calories: 25 Fat: 6
Fiber: 3
Carbs: 10
Protein: 1

35. Swiss Chard And Wild Garlic Noodles

Preparation time: 10 minutes
Cooking time: 20 minutes
Servings: 2
Ingredients:
- 150 g Greek yogurt, 10% fat content
- 1 small bunch of wild garlic
- 1 tbsp. pink pepper berries
- 1 tbsp. lemon juice
- 3 tbsp. olive oil
- Salt and sugar
- 200 g Swiss chard
- 200 g buckwheat spaghetti *
- 2 tbsp. water

Directions:
1. Remove the yogurt from the refrigerator. Clean the wild garlic and remove the coarse stalks. Finely puree the leaves with a little pink pepper, yoghurt, lemon juice and olive oil in a blender. Season the yogurt with salt and a pinch of sugar.
2. Clean the chard cut the white stems from the leaves in a wedge shape and dice. Cut the green into strips.

3. Set two liters of water to the boil in a saucepan, add two teaspoons of salt and the pasta and stir once and cook the pasta until al dente for about ten minutes.
4. While the pasta is cooking, bring the remaining oil to temperature in a pan. Add the diced chard stalks and fry for two minutes. Attach water and steam the stems covered for two to three minutes until soft. Attach the chard leaves and cook for another two minutes. Season with salt to taste.
5. Pour the noodles into a sieve and let them drain for about half a minute, then mix with the chard and divide into two deep plates. Pour the wild garlic yoghurt over it and serve everything.

Nutrition:
Calories: 32 Fat: 5 Fiber: 2
Carbs: 11 Protein: 4

36. Chanterelle Gratin

Preparation time: 10 minutes Cooking time: 20 minutes Servings: 4
Ingredients:
- 2 shallots
- 400 g chanterelles
- 200 g young, tender nettle leaves
- 200 g young spinach leaves
- 100 g cream
- salt and pepper
- freshly grated nutmeg
- 80 g grated parmesan cheese
- 2 cloves of garlic
- 2 tbsp. butter
- 100 ml milk
- 2 eggs

Directions:

1. Set the oven to 200 C. Remove the shell and chop the shallots and garlic. Clean the mushrooms, just rub them with a brush or with damp kitchen paper.
2. Place the nettles on the worktop (use disposable gloves), roll with the rolling pin. In this way the nettles will be broken and will not cause pain. Remove all stems. Clean and dry the nettles and spinach, then chop.
3. Dissolve a tablespoon of butter. Steam the shallots without letting them turn color. Add the garlic and let the mushrooms follow too. Sauté everything for about three to four minutes while stirring then mix in the nettles and spinach, pepper.
4. Set a casserole dish with butter and pour the contents of the pan into it. Bring the cream and milk to temperature in a saucepan, mix in the eggs, season with a little salt, pepper and nutmeg to taste. Spread the sauce over the mushroom mixture, sprinkle with a little Parmesan and bake in the oven on the middle rack for about a quarter of an hour until the surface has a crust.

Nutrition:
Calories: 12 Fat: 5 Fiber: 1 Carbs: 4 Protein: 4

37. Pumpkin Tortilla

Preparation time: 10 minutes
Cooking time: 20 minutes Servings: 4
Ingredients:

- 1 butternut squash (800 g)
- 2 onions
- 1 green pepper
- 0.5 frets of parsley
- 4 tbsp. olive oil
- salt and pepper
- 8 eggs
- 150 ml milk
- 100 g grated manchego
- noble sweet paprika powder

Directions:

1. Clean the pumpkin and cut lengthways in two. Scrape out the seeds and fibers. Cut the pumpkin halves into wedges and remove the skin. Cut the pumpkin flesh into one-centimeter cubes. Detach the skin from the onions and dice finely. Divide the pepper into quarters, remove the seeds and cut into

strips. Wash the parsley, shake dry, pluck the leaves and chop.

2. Warmth the oven to a temperature of 180. Bring the oil to a suitable temperature in a non-stick pan (about 26 centimeters in diameter). Fry the pumpkin cubes, turning them occasionally, over medium to high heat for about three minutes. Attach the onions and peppers and cook for another five to eight minutes. Salt and pepper everything individually to taste.
3. Meanwhile mix the eggs, milk, cheese and parsley together. Season with salt, pepper and the paprika powder.
4. Pour the mixed milk over the vegetables and let set in the hot oven (on medium level) for about a quarter of an hour.
5. Let the omelet rest briefly. Overturn on a plate, cut into pieces. Green salad goes well with it.

Nutrition:
Calories: 13
Fat: 3
Fiber: 12
Carbs: 4
Protein: 2

38. Pumpkin And Bean Vegetables

Preparation time: 10 minutes
Cooking time: 15 minutes
Servings: 4
Ingredients:

- 500 g nutmeg squash
- 1 onion
- 2 cloves of garlic
- 1 tbsp. olive oil
- 1 tbsp. butter
- salt and pepper
- 1 teaspoon turmeric
- 1 teaspoon ground cumin
- 1 teaspoon hot paprika powder
- 150 ml vegetable stock
- 400 g green beans
- 1 tbsp. lemon juice

Directions:

1. Remove the seeds from the pumpkin, remove the skin, cut into wedges, then cut into cubes one to two centimeters in size. Skin and finely dice the onion and garlic.

2. Bring the oil and butter to temperature in a pan. Sauté the onions until translucent over medium heat.

3. Add the garlic and pumpkin, sauté for three minutes, salt and pepper. Dust with the turmeric, cumin and paprika powder. Deglaze with the broth and simmer covered for a quarter of an hour over medium heat.

4. Meanwhile, clean the beans, cut them in half and blanch them in boiling salted water for about five to seven minutes, drain, rinse and drain.

5. Mix the beans with the pumpkin vegetables and cook for two to three minutes. Season the vegetables with lemon juice, salt and pepper.

Nutrition:
Calories: 21 Fat: 4 Fiber: 2 Carbs: 11 Protein: 4

39. Wok Vegetables With Tofu

Preparation time: 10 minutes
Cooking time: 15 minutes Servings: 4
Ingredients:

- 1 organic lemon
- 8 stalks of mint
- 3 centimeters of fresh ginger
- 1 red chili pepper
- 4 tbsp. neutral oil
- salt
- 400 g broad green beans
- 2 red peppers
- 2 spring onions
- 400 g tofu
- 150 ml vegetable stock, instant

Directions:

1. Wash and dry the lemon, rub the peel. Clean and dry the mint and remove the leaves.

Remove the peel from the ginger and cut. Clean the chili pepper, remove the seeds. Finely chop the mint, ginger and chili. Mix with the zest of the lemon, a tablespoon of oil and the salt.

2. Clean the beans and remove the end pieces, cut the beans diagonally into pieces just under one centimeter wide. Boil enough water in a saucepan, season with salt and boil the beans for about two minutes. Pour into a sieve, pour cold water over it and allow draining. Clean the peppers, cut into quarters and remove the seeds and the walls. Cut the quarters of the peppers into strips. Set and wash the spring onions and cut into rings. Drain the tofu and dice it an inch.

3. Bring the wok to temperature and add oil. Add the tofu, season with salt and fry for about four minutes until crispy. Add the vegetables and onions and stir-fry for about three minutes. Fry the herb paste, add the stock and season with salt. Serve the vegetables immediately. Rice or Asian noodles go well with it.

Nutrition:
Calories: 43 Fat: 11 Fiber: 8 Carbs: 21 Protein: 5

40. Pumpkin And Mushroom Curry

Preparation time: 10 minutes
Cooking time: 15 minutes
Servings: 2
Ingredients:

- 0.5 Hokkaido pumpkin (400 g)
- 250 g small mushrooms
- 1 onion
- 2 inches of ginger
- 2 tbsp. neutral oil
- 1 teaspoon curry paste, red or green
- 200 ml coconut milk
- 50 ml of water
- salt
- 2 teaspoons of lime juice, alternatively lemon juice
- 0.25 frets
- coriander

Directions:

1. Clean the pumpkin and scrape out the seeds and fibrous pulp. Cut the pumpkin with the skin into pieces about two centimeters in size. Clean the mushrooms, rub them with a

clean cloth and, depending on the size, leave them whole or cut in half. Remove the skin from the onion and ginger and cut into cubes.

2. Bring the oil to temperature in a saucepan and fry the mushrooms over medium heat. Add the pieces of pumpkin and fry briefly. Add the onion and ginger.

3. Mix the curry paste into the vegetables and fry briefly. Pour in the coconut milk and about 60 ml of water. Season the dish with salt and the juice of the lime and cook covered.

4. Meanwhile, clean and dry the coriander, remove the leaves and chop up. Flavor the curry with salt and sprinkle with the coriander.

Nutrition:

Calories: 15

Fat: 5

Fiber: 13

Carbs: 23

Protein: 3

41. Herbal Frittata With Peppers And Feta

Preparation time: 10 minutes

Cooking time: 15 minutes

Servings: 4

Ingredients:

- 5 eggs
- sea-salt
- 1 bunch of parsley
- 4 tbsp. freshly grated parmesan
- 2 red peppers
- 1 yellow pepper
- 150 g feta
- 3 tbsp. olive oil
- salt and pepper

Directions:

1. Mix the eggs in a bowl with a pinch of sea salt. Clean and dry the parsley, peel off the leaves and chop. Stir the parsley and parmesan into the eggs. Divide the peppers lengthways, clean, wash and cut into strips. Crumble the feta.

2. Bring the olive oil to temperature in a pan. Add the paprika strips and steam for about two minutes, season with a little salt and pepper. Stream the egg mixture over it and spread the feta on top. Cover and let the frittata stand for six to eight minutes over a

moderate heat. Slide on a platter, cut into pieces and serve warm or cold.

Nutrition:

Calories: 32

Fat: 5

Fiber: 2

Carbs: 11

Protein: 4

42. Vegetable Coconut Curry

Preparation time: 10 minutes

Cooking time: 20 minutes

Servings: 4

Ingredients:

- 300 g pointed cabbage
- 300 g Swiss chard
- 300 g broccoli
- 2 spring onions
- 4 centimeters of fresh ginger
- 4 stalks of basil
- 1 organic lime
- 2 tbsp. neutral oil
- salt
- 1 teaspoon of red or green curry paste
- 400 g coconut milk, pack or can

Directions:

1. Clean the vegetable parts. Cut the strong ribs flatter in the middle of the pointed cabbage. Cut the cabbage and the chard into strips one centimeter wide. Divide the broccoli, peel the stem and cut into slices about five millimeters thick.

2. Set and wash the spring onions and cut into rings. Remove the peel from the ginger and cut it first into slices, then into fine strips. Clean and dry the basil, peel off the leaves and chop. Wash the lime with hot water and dry, rub the peel and squeeze out the juice.

3. Set the oil to temperature in a large pan. Pour in the vegetables, add a little salt and fry over high to medium heat for three to four minutes until al dente. Attach the spring onions and ginger and fry. Stir in the curry paste. Pour in the coconut milk and bring to the boil once.

4. Season the curry with the peel of the lime, two to three tablespoons of lime juice and a little salt.

5. Sprinkle with the basil and serve. It is best to serve fragrant rice and a cucumber salad.

Nutrition:
Calories: 12
Fat: 11   Fiber: 9
Carbs: 25   Protein: 4

43. Wok Ratatouille

Preparation time: 10 minutes
Cooking time: 15 minutes
Servings: 2
Ingredients:

- 1 zucchini (200 g)
- 0.5 small eggplants (150 g)
- 1 red pepper
- 100 g cherry tomatoes
- 4 sprigs of thyme
- 1 sprig of rosemary
- 2 cloves of garlic
- 3 tbsp. olive oil
- salt and pepper

Directions:

1. Clean and trim the vegetables. Cut the zucchini, aborigine and bell pepper separately into half a centimeter cubes. Cut the tomatoes in half. Clean and dry the herbs and remove the needles and leaves and chop. Remove the garlic from the skin and cut into cubes.
2. Bring the wok to temperature and add two tablespoons of oil. Fry the eggplant cubes over high heat for two to three minutes while stirring. Add the zucchini and bell pepper with the remaining oil and herbs and stir-fry all ingredients for another two to three minutes.
3. Mix in the tomatoes and garlic and fry briefly. Season the dish with salt and pepper

and serve immediately. Fresh baguette is served with it.

Nutrition:
Calories: 13
Fat: 21
Fiber: 14
Carbs: 32
Protein: 9

44. Tofu With Curry Mushrooms

Preparation time: 10 minutes
Cooking time: 20 minutes
Servings: 4
Ingredients:

- 500 g mushrooms, or Egerlinge
- 2 spring onions
- 2 cloves of garlic
- 0.5 frets of parsley
- 0.5 organic lemon
- 2 teaspoons of coriander seeds
- 4 tbsp. neutral oil
- 2 teaspoons of hot curry powder
- 200 ml plant cream, preferably almond or oat cream
- salt and pepper
- 500 g tofu

Directions:

1. Rub the mushrooms with kitchen paper and remove the ends of the stems. Cut the mushrooms into slices. Clean and clean the spring onions and cut into rings.
2. Remove the garlic from the skin and cut into thin slices. Clean, dry and finely chop the parsley. Wash and dry half of the lemon with hot water, finely grate the peel, squeeze out a tablespoon of juice.
3. Heat a large saucepan. Roast the coriander in it for about a minute while stirring, then remove and finely pound in a mortar.
4. Bring two tablespoons of oil to temperature in the saucepan. In it, stir-fry the mushrooms over high heat for about four minutes until the liquid has evaporated again. Attach the onions and garlic and fry briefly. Dust the curry powder over it, also fry a little. Set in the cream and bring to the boil. Season the mushrooms with the coriander, lemon zest and lemon juice, salt and pepper to taste, then keep warm.

5. Slice the tofu into thin slices and season with salt and pepper to taste. Heat the remaining oil in a large pan. Attach the tofu slices and fry for about four minutes on each side over high heat. Mix the parsley with the mushrooms. Serve with the tofu.

Nutrition:
Calories: 21 Fat: 13 Fiber: 5 Carbs: 10 Protein: 9

45. Zucchini And Avocado Pasta

Preparation time: 20 minutes
Cooking time: 15 minutes
Servings: 4
Ingredients:

- Zucchini (1000 g)
- 3 avocados
- 200 ml rice-cream substitute
- 250 g cherry tomatoes
- 3 tbsp. olive oil
- 1 tbsp. powdered sugar
- salt and pepper
- 2 small cloves of garlic
- 4 tbsp. lemon juice
- 1 bunch of parsley

Directions:

1. Set and clean the zucchini and cut into spaghetti-like strips with the spiral cutter. Halve and stone the avocados. Detach the pulp from the skin with a spoon and place in a tall mixing bowl with the rice-cream substitute. Puree with the hand blender. Set aside the avocado cream.
2. Wash the tomatoes and pat dry. Warmth 1 tablespoon of oil in a pan. Add the tomatoes, sprinkle with powdered sugar and caramelize over high heat and let them pop. Set with salt and pepper and keep warm.
3. Peel and finely dice the garlic. Heat the remaining oil in a large pan and sauté the garlic until light yellow. Add the zucchini spaghetti and cook over a medium heat for about 5 minutes while stirring. Stir in the avocado cream. Simmer everything over low to medium heat for 2–4 minutes while stirring. Season with salt, pepper and lemon juice. Stir in the tomatoes.
4. Wash the parsley and shake dry. Pluck the leaves, chop and stir into the zucchini and avocado pasta. Spread the pasta on the plates.

Nutrition:
Calories: 13
Fat: 8
Fiber: 4
Carbs: 14
Protein: 8

46. Paleo Beef Soup

Preparation time: 1 hour minutes
Cooking time: 20 minutes Servings: 6
Ingredients:

- 1 lb. beef, ground
- 1 lb. sausage, sliced
- 4 cups beef stock
- 30 oz. canned tomatoes, diced
- 1 green bell pepper, chopped
- 3 zucchinis, chopped
- 1 cup celery, chopped
- 1 tsp. Italian seasoning
- 1/2 yellow onion, chopped
- 1/2 teaspoon oregano, dried
- 1/2 teaspoon basil, dried
- 1/4 teaspoon garlic powder
- Salt and black pepper to the taste

Directions:

1. Cook until it browns and drains excess fat.
2. Add tomatoes, zucchini, bell pepper, celery, onion, Italian seasoning, basil, oregano, garlic powder, salt, pepper to the taste and the stock, stir, bring to a boil, reduce heat to medium-low and simmer for 1 hour. Enjoy!

Nutrition:
Calories: 370 Fat: 17g
Carbs: 35g
Protein: 25g Fiber: 10g
Sugar: 0g

47. Paleo Roasted Carrots

Preparation time: 15 minutes
Cooking time: 40 minutes
Servings: 4
Ingredients:

- 1 and 1/2 pounds young carrots (yellow, purple and red ones)
- 2 tbsp. balsamic vinegar
- 2 garlic cloves, finely minced
- 2 tbsp. ghee
- 1 tbsp. honey
- Salt and black pepper to taste
- A handful parsley leaves, finely chopped

Directions:

1. In a bowl, mix vinegar with ghee, honey, garlic, salt, and pepper to the taste and stir very well.
2. Add carrots and toss to coat.
3. Transfer this to a baking dish, introduce in the oven at 400 degrees and bake for 30 minutes.
4. Take carrots out of the oven, sprinkle parsley on top, toss gently and serve right away as a side dish.
5. Enjoy!

Nutrition:
Calories: 40
Fat: 6g
Carbs: 20g
Protein: 2g
Fiber: 1g
Sugar: 1g

48. Paleo Glazed Salmon

Preparation time: 15 minutes
Cooking time: 25 minutes
Servings: 4
Ingredients:

- 2 tbsp. pure maple syrup
- 4 salmon fillets, skin-on
- Salt and white pepper to taste
- 2 tsp. Dijon mustard
- Juice and zest from 1 orange
- 2 garlic cloves, finely chopped

Directions:

1. In a bowl, mix maple syrup with orange zest, juice, mustard, salt, pepper and garlic and whisk well.
2. Arrange salmon in a baking dish, brush with the maple syrup and orange mix, set in the oven at 400 F and bake.

3. Divide between plates and serve right away.
4. Enjoy!

Nutrition
Calories: 190
Fat: 10g
Carbs: 12g
Protein: 26g
Fiber: 0.6g
Sugar: 0g

49. Paleo Lobster With Sauce

Preparation time: 5 minutes
Cooking time: 20 minutes
Servings: 4
Ingredients:

- 1/4 cup ghee, melted
- 4 lobster tails
- Salt and black pepper to taste
- 2 tbsp. Sriracha sauce
- 1 tbsp. lime juice
- 1 tbsp. chives, chopped
- Some parsley leaves, chopped for serving

Directions:

1. In a bowl, mix Sriracha sauce with ghee, chives, salt, pepper and lime juice and whisk well.
2. Cut lobster tails halfway through in the center, open with your fingers, fill them with half of the Sriracha mix, arrange on preheated grill over medium-high heat, cook for 4 minutes, flip and cook for 3 minutes more.
3. Divide lobster tails on plates, drizzle the rest of the Sriracha sauce, sprinkle parsley on top and serve.
4. Enjoy!

Nutrition
Calories: 240 Fat: 16g
Carbs: 2g Protein: 19g
Fiber: 0.5g Sugar: 0g

50. Paleo Steamed Clams

Preparation time: 5 minutes
Cooking time: 20 minutes
Servings: 4
Ingredients:

- 3 tbsp. ghee
- 1 and 1/2 lb. shell clams, scrubbed
- 1/4 cup white wine
- 3 garlic cloves, finely chopped
- Salt and black pepper to taste
- 1/2 cup chicken stock
- 2 tbsp. parsley, chopped
- Lemon wedges

Directions:
1. Set up a pot with the ghee over medium heat, add garlic, stir and cook for 1 minute.
2. Add stock and clams, cover pot and cook for 4-5 minutes.
3. Divide clams on plates, sprinkle parsley on top, salt, and pepper and serve with lemon wedges on the side.
4. Enjoy!

Nutrition
Calories: 79
Fat: 23g
Carbs: 9g
Protein: 22g
Fiber: 0.4g
Sugar: 0g

51. Paleo Salmon Pie

Preparation time: 20 minutes
Cooking time: 1 hour
Servings: 4
Ingredients:

- 8 sweet potatoes, thinly sliced
- 4 cups salmon, already cooked and shredded
- 1 red onion, chopped
- 2 carrots, chopped
- 1 celery stalk, chopped
- Salt and black pepper to taste
- 2 tbsp. chives, chopped
- 2 cups coconut milk
- 1 tbsp. tapioca starch
- 2 garlic cloves, minced

- 3 tbsp. ghee

Directions:
1. Set up a pan with the ghee over medium heat, add garlic and tapioca, stir and cook for 1 minute.
2. Add coconut milk, stir and cook for 3 minutes.
3. Add salt and pepper and stir again.
4. In a bowl, mix carrots with salmon, celery, chives, onion, salt, and pepper to the taste and stir well.
5. Add half of the salmon combination, the rest of the potatoes and top with the remaining sauce.
6. Introduce in the oven at 375 degrees and bake for 1 hour.
7. Divide between plates and serve hot.
8. Enjoy!

Nutrition
Calories: 260 Fat: 11g
Carbs: 20g Protein: 14g
Fiber: 12g Sugar: 0g

52. Paleo Grilled Calamari

Preparation time: 20 minutes
Cooking time: 15 minutes
Servings: 4
Ingredients:

- 2 lb. calamari, tentacles, and tubes sliced into rings
- 1 lime, sliced
- lemon, sliced
- 1 orange, sliced
- 2 tbsp. parsley, chopped
- Salt and black pepper to taste
- 3 tbsp. lemon juice
- 1/4 cup extra virgin olive oil
- 2 garlic cloves, minced

Directions:

1. In a bowl, mix calamari with sliced lemon, lime, orange, lemon juice, salt, pepper, parsley, garlic and olive oil and toss to coat.
2. Heat up your kitchen grill over medium high heat, add calamari and fruits slices, cook for 5 minutes, divide between plates and serve.
3. Enjoy!

Nutrition
Calories: 90 Fat: 3g
Carbs: 0.2g Protein: 15g
Fiber: 0g Sugar: 0g

53. Paleo Shrimp And Zucchini Noodles

Preparation time: 20 minutes
Cooking time: 25 minutes
Servings: 2
Ingredients:

- 2 zucchinis, sliced in thin noodles
- 1 lb. shrimp, peeled and deveined
- 4 garlic cloves, minced
- Salt and black pepper to taste
- 1/4 cup white wine
- 2 tbsp. chives, chopped
- 2 tbsp. lemon juice
- 2 tbsp. coconut oil

Directions:

1. Heat up a pan with the coconut oil over medium-high heat, add garlic, stir and cook for 3 minutes.
2. Add shrimp, stir and cook for 3 minutes and transfer them to a plate.
3. Pour lemon juice and wine into the pan, bring to a boil over medium heat and simmer for a few moments.
4. Add zucchini noodles, the shrimp, salt, and pepper to the taste stir gently and divide among plates. Sprinkle chives on top and serve. Enjoy!

Nutrition
Calories: 140 Fat: 12g
Carbs: 6g Protein: 18g
Fiber: 3g Sugar: 0g

54. Paleo Scallops With Delicious Puree

Preparation time: 20 minutes
Cooking time: 25 minutes Servings: 2
Ingredients:

- 3 garlic cloves, minced
- 2 cups cauliflower florets, chopped
- 2 cups sweet potatoes, chopped
- 2 rosemary springs
- 12 sea scallops
- Salt and black pepper to taste
- 1/4 cup pine nuts, toasted
- 2 cups veggie stock
- 2 tbsp. extra virgin olive oil
- A handful chives, chopped

Directions:

1. Put cauliflower, potatoes, and stock in a pot, bring to a boil over medium-high heat, reduce temperature and simmer until veggies are soft.
2. Drain veggies, transfer them to your blender, add salt and pepper to the taste and pulse until you obtain a puree.
3. Warmth up a pan with the oil over medium-high heat, add rosemary and garlic, stir and cook for 1 minute.
4. Add scallops, cook them for 2 minutes, often stirring, season them with salt and pepper to the taste and take them off heat.
5. Divide puree on small plates, arrange scallops on top, sprinkle chives and pine nuts at the end and serve.
6. Enjoy!

Nutrition
Calories: 170
Fat: 10g
Carbs: 2g
Protein: 22g
Fiber: 0g
Sugar: 0g

55. Paleo Salmon With Avocado Sauce

Preparation time: 20 minutes
Cooking time: 25 minutes Servings: 2
Ingredients:

- 1 tsp. cumin
- 1 tsp. sweet paprika
- 1 tsp. chili powder
- 1 tsp. onion powder
- 1/2 tsp. garlic powder
- 2 lb. salmon filets, cut into four pieces
- Salt and black pepper to taste

For the avocado sauce:

- 2 avocados, pitted, peeled and chopped
- 1 garlic clove, minced
- Juice from 1 lime
- 1 red onion, chopped
- 1 tbsp. extra virgin olive oil
- Salt and black pepper to taste
- 1 tbsp. cilantro, finely chopped

Directions:

1. In a bowl, mix paprika with cumin, onion powder, garlic powder, chili powder, salt and pepper to the taste. Add salmon pieces, toss to coat and keep in the fridge for 20 minutes.
2. Put avocado in a bowl and mash well with a fork. Add red onion, garlic clove, lime juice, olive oil, chopped cilantro, salt, and pepper to the taste and stir very well.
3. Take salmon out of the fridge, place it on preheated grill over medium-high heat and cook it for 3 minutes. Flip salmon, cook for three more minutes and divide on serving plates.
4. Top each salmon piece with avocado sauce and serve. Enjoy!

Nutrition
Calories: 150

Fat: 12g
Carbs: 9g
Protein: 24g
Fiber: 6g
Sugar: 0g

56. Paleo Fish Tacos

Preparation time: 20 minutes Cooking time: 25 minutes Servings: 4
Ingredients:

- 4 tilapia fillets, cut into medium pieces
- 1/4 cup coconut flour
- 2 eggs
- 3/4 cup tapioca starch
- 1/2 cup tapioca starch
- 1/4 cup sparkling water
- 2 cups cabbage, shredded
- 2 cups coconut oil
- Salt and black pepper to taste
- Lime wedges for serving
- Cauliflower tortillas

For the Pico de Gallo:

- 2 tomatoes, chopped
- 2 tbsp. jalapeños, finely chopped
- 6 tbsp. yellow onion, finely chopped
- 2 tbsp. lime juice
- 1 tbsp. cilantro, finely chopped
- Salt to taste

For the mayo:

- 1 tbsp. Sriracha sauce
- 1/4 cup homemade mayonnaise
- 2 tsp. lime juice

Directions:

1. In a bowl, mix tomatoes with tomatoes with onion, jalapeño, cilantro, two tablespoons lime juice and salt to the taste, stir well, cover and keep in the fridge for now.
2. In another bowl, mix mayo with Sriracha and two teaspoons lime juice, stir well, cover and also keep in the refrigerator. In a bowl, combine 3/4 cup tapioca starch with coconut flour, sparkling water, salt, pepper and eggs and whisk very well. Put the rest of the tapioca starch in a separate bowl. Pat dry tapioca pieces, coat with tapioca starch and dip each piece in eggs mix.
3. Heat up a pan with the coconut oil over medium-high heat, transfer fish fillets to pan, cook for 1 minute, flip them, cook for one

more minute, transfer to paper towels and drain excess fat.

4. Arrange tortillas on a working surface, divide cabbage on them, add a piece of fish on each, add some of the Pico de Gallo and top with mayo. Serve with lime wedges. Enjoy!

Nutrition

Calories: 230   Fat: 10g
Carbs: 12g   Protein: 13g
Fiber: 4g   Sugar: 0g

57. Smoked Salmon And Fresh Veggies

Preparation time: 20 minutes
Cooking time: 10 minutes
Servings: 2
Ingredients:

- 2 cups cherry tomatoes, cut in halves
- 1 red onion, thinly sliced
- 8 ounces smoked salmon, thinly sliced
- 1 cucumber, thinly chopped
- 6 tbsp. extra virgin olive oil
- 1/2 tsp. garlic, minced
- 2 tbsp. lemon juice
- Salt and black pepper to taste
- 1 tsp. balsamic vinegar
- Some dill, finely chopped
- 1/2 tsp. oregano, dried

Directions:

1. In a bowl, mix oil with garlic, balsamic vinegar, oregano and garlic and whisk well.
2. Attach salt and pepper to taste and stir well again.
3. In a bowl, mix cucumber with tomatoes and onion.
4. Drizzle the dressing over veggies and toss to coat.
5. Roll salmon pieces and divide them among plates.
6. Add mixed veggies on the side, sprinkle dill all over and serve.
7. Enjoy!

Nutrition

Calories: 159
Fat: 23g
Carbs: 2g
Protein: 14g
Fiber: 3g
Sugar: 0g

58. Paleo Roasted Trout

Preparation time: 5 minutes
Cooking time: 30 minutes
Servings: 4
Ingredients:

- 3 trout, cleaned and gutted
- 1 bunch dill
- 2 lemons, sliced
- 1 bunch rosemary
- 2 fennel bulbs, sliced
- Salt and black pepper
- 2 tbsp. extra virgin olive oil

Directions:

1. Grease a baking dish with some oil, spread fennel slices on the bottom and add trout after you've set them with salt and pepper.
2. Fill each fish with lemon slices, dill and rosemary springs.
3. Top fish with the rest of the herbs and lemon slices, drizzle the rest of the oil, introduce everything in the oven at 500 degrees and bake for 10 minutes.
4. Leave fish to cool down, divide between plates and serve.
5. Enjoy!

Nutrition

Calories: 143
Fat: 2.3g
Carbs: 1g
Protein: 6g
Fiber: 0g
Sugar: 0g

59. Paleo Roasted Cod

Preparation time: 20 minutes
Cooking time: 30 minutes
Servings: 4
Ingredients:

- 1/4 cup ghee
- 4 medium cod fillets, skinless
- 2 garlic cloves, minced
- 1 tbsp. parsley leaves, finely chopped
- 1 tsp. mustard
- 1 shallot, finely chopped
- 3 tbsp. prosciutto, chopped
- 2 tbsp. lemon juice
- 2 tbsp. coconut oil
- Salt and black pepper

- Lemon wedges for platter

Directions:

1. In a bowl, merge parsley with ghee, mustard, garlic, shallot, prosciutto, salt, pepper and lemon juice and whisk very well.
2. Set up an oven proof pan with the coconut oil over medium-high heat, add fish, season with salt and pepper to the taste and cook for 4 minutes on each side.
3. Spread ghee mix over fish, introduce in the oven at 425 degrees and bake for 10 minutes.
4. Set between plates and serve with lemon wedges on the side.
5. Enjoy!

Nutrition

Calories: 138

Fat: 4g

Carbs: 1g

Protein: 23g

Fiber: 0g

Sugar: 0g

60. Superb Tuna Dish

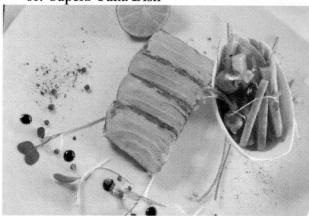

Preparation time: 20 minutes

Cooking time: 25 minutes

Servings: 2

Ingredients:

- 1 tsp. fennel seeds
- 1 tsp. mustard seeds
- 4 medium tuna steaks
- 1/4 tsp. black peppercorns
- Salt and black pepper to taste
- 4 tbsp. sesame seeds
- 3 tbsp. coconut oil

Directions:

1. In your grinder, mix peppercorns with fennel and mustard seeds and grind well.
2. Attach sesame seeds, salt, and pepper to the taste and grind again well.
3. Spread this mix on a plate, add tuna steaks and toss to coat.
4. Warmth up a pan with the oil over medium-high heat, add tuna steaks and cook for 3 minutes on each side.
5. Enjoy!

Nutrition

Calories: 240

Fat: 2g

Carbs: g

Protein: 53g

Fiber: 0g

Sugar: 0g

CHAPTER 7

Dinner

61. Broccoli Wraps

Preparation time: 15 minutes Cooking time: 20 minutes Servings: 4

Ingredients:

- 1 head broccoli, cut into florets - 3 eggs
- 3 garlic cloves, finely minced
- 1 shallot, minced - 1 teaspoon chopped fresh chives
- 1 teaspoon dried oregano
- 1 teaspoon chopped fresh parsley - 1 teaspoon salt
- Freshly ground black pepper

Directions:

1. Preheat the oven to 350F.
2. In a food processor, press the broccoli until roughly chopped (don't over process—you want it to still be rough). Set to a microwave-safe bowl, and microwave on high for 2 minutes. Allow to cool for a few minutes, and then twist in a thin cloth or cheesecloth to remove any water (not a lot will come out, but the little that's there needs to be removed). Transfer the broccoli to a medium bowl. In a small bowl, merge together the eggs, garlic, shallot, chives, oregano, and parsley, and set with salt and pepper; whisk

over the broccoli, and mix until well incorporated.

3. Set a large baking sheet with parchment paper, and scoop the broccoli mixture into four equal sections. Spread each section of broccoli out until it's about 1/4 inch thick, leaving a little room in between each. Bake and then flip and bake for another 7 minutes.
4. Detach the baking sheet from the oven, and allow the broccoli wraps to cool. Store in the refrigerator. To reheat, broil them quickly in the oven or toaster oven.

Nutrition

Calories: 143 Fat: 2.3g Carbs: 1g

Protein: 6g Fiber: 0g Sugar: 0g

62. Steamed Broccoli With Hollandaise

Preparation time: 5 minutes
Cooking time: 15 minutes
Servings: 4
Ingredients:

- 1 large head broccoli
- 4 egg yolks
- 1 tablespoon freshly squeezed lemon juice
- 1/2 cup unsalted, grass-fed butter (1 full stick), melted
- 1/4 teaspoon ground cayenne pepper
- Salt

Directions:

1. Boil the broccoli. If you don't have a steamer addition for your saucepan, you can boil the broccoli for 1 to 11/2 minutes.
2. Set a saucepan of water to a simmer. To make the hollandaise sauce, in a heatproof bowl that will fit over the saucepan (without the bottom touching the water), quickly whisk the egg yolks and lemon juice together until the mixture becomes frothy and starts to expand, about 30 seconds. Set the bowl in the saucepan, and continue to whisk. Slowly

drizzle the melted butter in while stirring and continuing to whisk until the sauce has doubled in size, 3 to 4 minutes.

3. Remove from the heat, stir in the cayenne and a pinch of salt, and serve immediately or keep warm over a pan of warm (not hot) water until ready to serve.

Nutrition
Calories: 240 Fat: 16g
Carbs: 2g Protein: 19g
Fiber: 0.5g Sugar: 0g

63. Bacon-Broccoli Bites

Preparation time: 15 minutes
Cooking time: 30 minutes Servings: 4
Ingredients:

- 1 large head broccoli, cut into florets
- 1 onion, diced
- 3 garlic cloves, minced
- 3 slices bacon, cooked and chopped
- 3 eggs, whisked
- Salt
- Freshly ground black pepper
- Coconut oil, for greasing

Directions:

1. Preheat the oven to 350F.
2. Set a large saucepan with salted water to a boil. Attach the broccoli florets, and cook. Strain really well, and allow them to cool slightly.
3. In a food processor or blender, press the broccoli, onion, and garlic until pretty finely chopped. Set the mixture to a medium bowl, and stir to merge with the bacon and eggs. Season with salt and pepper.
4. Drip a mini-muffin tin with a paper towel dipped in coconut oil. Scoop the broccoli mixture into each muffin cup. If there's any

leftover egg at the bottom of your bowl, pour it over the broccoli bites. Bake until set, and serve.

Nutrition
Calories: 190
Fat: 10g
Carbs: 12g
Protein: 26g
Fiber: 0.6g
Sugar: 0g

64. Broccoli-Sweet Potato Hash

Preparation time: 10 minutes
Cooking time: 20 minutes
Servings: 4
Ingredients:

- 2 tablespoons grass-fed butter or ghee
- 1/2 onion, diced
- 1 garlic clove, minced
- 2 small sweet potatoes, peeled and diced
- 1/2 pound chorizo or Italian sausage
- 1 small head broccoli, finely chopped

Directions:

1. Dissolve the butter in a saucepan. Set the onion and garlic until the onion is slightly translucent, about 5 minutes. Add the sweet potatoes, and cook for another 5 minutes.
2. Attach the chorizo, break it up with a wooden spoon, and increase the heat to medium-high. Cook and bits of it begin to get crunchy and browned, another 5 minutes.Add the broccoli and stir. Cook and serve hot.

Nutrition
Calories: 138
Fat: 4g
Carbs: 1g
Protein: 23g
Fiber: 0g
Sugar: 0g

65. Pantry Basic: Homemade Nut Butter

Preparation time: 15 minutes
Cooking time: 0 minutes Servings: 2
Ingredients:

- 2 cups raw almonds (or the nut of your choice)
- 1 to 2 tablespoons coconut oil

Directions:

1. Merge all the ingredients in a food processor until the butter reaches the consistency you like this can take up to 15 minutes. Place in a jar in the refrigerator for up to two weeks.

Nutrition
Calories: 230 Fat: 10g Carbs: 12g
Protein: 13g Fiber: 4g Sugar: 0g

66. Zucchini-Noodle Salad With Lemon, Peas, And Cashews

Preparation time: 10 minutes, and 2 hours to dip
Cooking time: 0 minutes
Servings: 4
Ingredients:

- 1/4 cup uncooked cashews
- 1/2 cup water
- Salt (optional)
- Freshly ground black pepper (optional)
- 3 or 4 zucchini, spiralized or julienned into noodles
- 1/2 red bell pepper, diced
- 1/2 cup green peas
- 2 or 3 radishes, sliced
- 1/4 cup broccoli or broccoli florets
- Juice of 1 lemon
- 1/2 lemon, for garnish

Directions:

1. In a medium bowl, soak the cashews in the water for 2 hours, making sure there is enough water to cover them.
2. In a blender, merge the soaked cashews and soaking water to a creamy consistency. Season with salt and pepper (if using).
3. In a large bowl, stir well to merge the zucchini noodles, bell pepper, peas, radishes, broccoli, and lemon juice.
4. Plate the salad, drizzle with the cashew cream, garnish with lemon wedges, and serve.

Nutrition
Calories: 138
Fat: 4g

Carbs: 1g
Protein: 23g
Fiber: 0g
Sugar: 0g

67. Ratatouille

Preparation time: 15 minutes
Cooking time: 1 hour Servings: 4 Ingredients:

- 2 tablespoons extra-virgin olive oil, divided
- 3 garlic cloves, minced
- 1 eggplant, diced
- Salt
- Freshly ground black pepper
- 2 teaspoons dried parsley
- 2 zucchini, cut into rounds
- 1 onion, cut into rings
- 1 green bell pepper, cut into strips
- 2 large tomatoes, chopped (or 10 ounces cherry tomatoes, sliced)
- 1 or 2 tablespoons chopped fresh parsley, for garnish

Directions:

1. Preheat the oven to 350F.
2. Grease a baking dish with 1 tablespoon of olive oil. In a skillet over medium heat, warmth the remaining 1 tablespoon of olive oil. Sauté the garlic until fragrant, about 2 minutes, and add the eggplant. Cook, stirring periodically, until the eggplant begins to soften, about 10 minutes. Season with salt, pepper and the dried parsley.
3. Spread the eggplant across the bottom of a baking dish, and layer the zucchini rounds on top.
4. Season with salt, and layer in the onion, bell pepper, and tomatoes, seasoning each layer with a pinch of salt and some pepper.

5. Bake until the vegetables are tender. Garnish with the fresh parsley and serve.

Nutrition

Calories: 321 Fat: 11 g

Carbs: 5 g

Protein: 21 g Fiber: 3.5 g

Sugar: 1 g

68. Baked Zucchini Fries

Preparation time: 15 minutes

Cooking time: 25 minutes

Servings: 4-6

Ingredients:

- 2 large zucchini
- 1/2 cup almond flour
- 11/2 teaspoons garlic powder
- 11/2 teaspoons onion powder
- 2 eggs, whisked
- Salt
- Freshly ground black pepper

Directions:

1. Preheat the oven to 400F.
2. Chop the ends off the zucchini, and cut them in half widthwise, then lengthwise. Cut into French fry–like strips, and pat dry with a paper towel.
3. In a bowl, merge together the almond flour, garlic powder, and onion powder. Dip the zucchini fries in the egg, let any excess egg drip off, and toss them in the almond flour mixture. Season with salt and pepper.
4. Set the fries out on a baking sheet, put them in the oven, and immediately lower the heat to 350F.

5. Cook until the fries are crisp, checking on them halfway through the cooking time and lowering the heat if they're getting brown too quickly.
6. Serve immediately.

Nutrition:

Calories: 40

Fat: 6g

Carbs: 20g

Protein: 2g

Fiber: 1g

Sugar: 1g

69. Pad Thai

Preparation time: 10 minutes

Cooking time: 20 minutes

Servings: 4

Ingredients:

- 1 pound boneless skinless chicken breast
- 2 tablespoons coconut aminos
- 2 garlic cloves, minced
- 1 teaspoon grated fresh ginger
- 1 to 2 tablespoons almond butter
- 1 tablespoon freshly squeezed lime juice, plus 4 lime wedges for garnish
- 2 teaspoons fish sauce
- 1/2 teaspoon red pepper
- 2 large zucchini, spiralized or julienned into noodles
- 1 cup bean sprouts
- 1/3 cup slivered almonds
- 2 to 3 tablespoons chopped fresh cilantro, for garnish

Directions:

1. Set a pot of water, boil or steam the chicken breasts for about 15 minutes, or until they're cooked through. Pat dry and slice into bite-size pieces.

2. In a large bowl, mix the coconut aminos, garlic, ginger, almond butter, lime juice, fish sauce, and red pepper flakes. Set aside.
3. Set a large skillet over medium-low heat, gently sauté the zucchini until they just start to become tender. Detach from the heat, and mix in with the pad thai sauce. Stir in the chicken, and serve topped with bean sprouts, almonds, cilantro, and a wedge of lime.

Nutrition

Calories: 150

Fat: 12g

Carbs: 9g

Protein: 24g

Fiber: 6g

Sugar: 0g

70. Zucchini-Spinach Fritters

Preparation time: 5 minutes
Cooking time: 15 minutes
Servings: 4-6
Ingredients:

- 1 (14-ounce) can artichoke hearts, clear and chopped
- 12 ounces fresh spinach, washed, cooked, and drained
- 1 large zucchini, shredded
- 6 scallions, chopped
- 2 or 3 garlic cloves, minced
- 2 eggs, lightly beaten
- 1/2 cup almond flour
- 1 teaspoon salt
- 1 tablespoon extra-virgin olive oil

Directions:

1. With your hands, press as much liquid out of the artichoke hearts, spinach, and zucchini as possible.
2. In a food processor, merge the artichoke hearts, spinach, zucchini, scallions, and garlic until roughly chopped. Set the mixture to a large bowl, add the eggs and almond flour, and season with salt. Mix well.
3. Set a large nonstick sauté pan over medium-high heat, heat the olive oil. Drop heaping tablespoons of the mixture into the pan, and cook for 2 to 3 minutes on each side, flattening them a little with your spatula to make them into mini-pancake shapes.Serve immediately.

Nutrition:
Calories: 21
Fat: 4
Fiber: 2
Carbs: 11

Protein: 4

71. Emergency Pasta With Zoodles

Preparation time: 5 minutes
Cooking time: 5 minutes
Servings: 4
Ingredients:

- 1/4 cup extra-virgin olive oil
- 2 or 3 garlic cloves, thinly sliced
- 1/4 hot red pepper, minced (or 1/4 teaspoon red pepper flakes)
- 3 or 4 large zucchini, spiralized or julienned into noodles
- Salt
- Freshly ground black pepper

Directions:

1. In a large sauté pan over medium-low heat, heat the olive oil. Add the garlic, and stir it around. Detach from the heat as soon as the garlic becomes fragrant—about 30 seconds—because you don't want to burn it at all. Add the hot red pepper, and pour the sauce into a serving dish.
2. In the same pan over medium heat, sauté the zucchini noodles for 3 to 4 minutes, just until slightly softened. Transfer the noodles to the serving dish, season with salt and pepper, and toss with the sauce.
3. Serve immediately.

Nutrition:
Calories: 32
Fat: 3 g
Carbs: 12 g
Protein: 1 g
Fiber: 3 g
Sugar: 1.9 g

72. Zucchini Lasagna

Preparation time: 15 minutes
Cooking time: 1 hour and 15 minutes Servings: 6-8
Ingredients:

- 2 large zucchini
- 1 pound spicy Italian sausage
- 1 pound ground beef
- 1 onion, diced
- 1 small green bell pepper, diced
- 1 (16-ounce) can tomato sauce
- 1 cup tomato paste
- 1/4 cup red wine (optional; omit if strict Paleo)

- 2 tablespoons chopped fresh basil
- 2 tablespoons chopped fresh parsley
- 1 tablespoon chopped fresh oregano
- Salt
- Freshly ground black pepper
- 1 pound fresh mushrooms, sliced

Directions:
1. Preheat the oven to 325F.
2. With a vegetable peeler to cut the zucchini lengthwise into small, thin sheets that resemble lasagna.
3. Set a large skillet; cook the Italian sausage for 5 to 7 minutes per side, until browned. Remove from the skillet, and set aside. Attach the ground beef to the skillet, and cook for 5 minutes, using a wooden spoon to break up the beef. Attach the onion and bell pepper, and continue cooking until the beef is no longer pink, about another 5 minutes.
4. Whip in the tomato sauce, tomato paste, wine (if using), basil, parsley, and oregano, and season with salt and pepper. Once the sauce begins to boil, lessen the heat and simmer for 20 minutes, stirring frequently. Remove from the heat.
5. To assemble the lasagna, start by spreading half the meat sauce into the bottom of an 8-by-12-inch baking dish. Layer half the zucchini slices over the meat sauce. Add the Italian sausage and all the mushrooms. Continue layering the lasagna by adding the remaining meat sauce and zucchini sheets.
6. Seal with foil, and bake the lasagna for 45 minutes. Carefully remove the foil, raise the oven temperature to 375F, and bake for an additional 10 to 15 minutes.
7. Detach from the oven and allow to rest for 5 minutes before slicing. Serve warm.

Nutrition:
Calories: 21 Fat: 4 g Carbs: 14 g Protein: 3.1 g
Fiber: 2.7 g Sugar: 2.9 g

73. Zucchini-Noodle Ramen

Preparation time: 15 minutes
Cooking time: 2 hours and 15 minutes Servings: 4-6
Ingredients:

- 1 pound pork tenderloin
- 1 tablespoon salt
- 2 bunches scallions, divided
- 1 (1-inch) piece fresh ginger root, sliced
- 4 garlic cloves, crushed
- Toppings (optional): hardboiled eggs, kimchi, jalapeño peppers, fresh cilantro
- 5 tablespoons coconut aminos
- 2 tablespoons sake (optional; omit if strict Paleo)
- 11/2 tablespoons sesame oil
- 4 large zucchini, spiralized or julienned

Directions:
1. Season the pork with the salt, and refrigerate overnight.
2. Remove the pork from the refrigerator, and place in a large saucepan over medium-high heat. Add 11/2 bunches of scallions and the ginger and garlic to the pan with enough water to just cover the pork. Set to a boil, lower the heat, and simmer for at least 2 hours (although longer is better, if possible).
3. While the broth is cooking, prepare all your toppings (if using): Soft-boil the eggs (see here), slice the jalapeños and the remaining 1/2 bunch of scallions, and chop the cilantro.
4. Add the coconut aminos, sake (if using), and sesame oil to the broth. Continue to simmer, and add the zucchini noodles about 5 minutes before you're ready to serve.
5. Transfer the pork to a platter, slice it, and transfer it back to the saucepan. Serve the

ramen with whichever toppings sound good
to you.
Nutrition:
Calories: 21 Fat: 5 g Carbs: 11 g Protein: 1 g Fiber:
5 g Sugar: 0.3 g

74. Stuffed Zucchini Boats

Preparation time: 10 minutes
Cooking time: 1 hour Servings: 4
Ingredients:

- 4 large zucchini
- 1 pound ground beef
- 2 tablespoons extra-virgin olive oil
- 1 onion, diced
- 2 garlic cloves, chopped
- Salt
- Freshly ground black pepper
- 3/4 cup green olives, roughly chopped
- 2 hardboiled eggs, chopped

Directions:

1. Preheat the oven to 350F.
2. Cut the zucchini lengthwise, and scoop the insides out with a spoon. Chop the inside parts, and add them to a medium bowl with the ground beef. In a skillet over medium-high warmth, heat the olive oil. Sauté the onion and garlic until the onion is slightly translucent, about 5 minutes. Add the ground beef–zucchini mixture, and cook for about 5 minutes more, until completely browned, breaking the meat up as you cook it. Season with salt and pepper.
3. Detach the skillet from the heat, and add the olives and hardboiled eggs. Stir well.
4. Stuff the zucchini boats with the meat mixture, and place them on a baking sheet. Bake for 45 minutes, until tender, and serve.

Nutrition:
Calories: 17
Fat: 5 g
Carbs: 12 g
Protein: 1 g
Fiber: 3 g
Sugar: 1.3 g

75. Stuffed Squash

Preparation time: 10 minutes
Cooking time: 1 hour
Servings: 2
Ingredients:

- 2 round squash, such as acorn or 8-ball zucchini
- 2 tablespoons extra-virgin olive oil
- Salt
- Freshly ground black pepper
- 1/2 teaspoon onion powder
- 1/2 onion, diced
- 1 pound ground beef
- 11/2 teaspoons garlic powder
- 11/2 teaspoons dried oregano
- 1/8 teaspoon red pepper flakes
- 1 (14.5-ounce) can diced tomatoes, drained
- 1 or 2 tablespoons chopped fresh basil or oregano

Directions:

1. Preheat the oven to 350F.
2. Carefully cut the tops off the squash, scoop out the seeds, trim the bottoms if necessary so they will stand up straight, and season the insides with the olive oil, salt, pepper, and onion powder. Roast for 45 minutes.
3. While the squash are in the oven, in a large sauté pan over medium heat, sauté the onion until slightly translucent, about 5 minutes. Add the beef, and break it up with a wooden spoon. Season with the garlic powder, oregano, red pepper flakes, and some more salt and pepper.
4. Once the beef is no longer pink, 7 to 8 minutes, reduce the heat to low and add the tomatoes. Continue to simmer until the squash have finished cooking.
5. To serve, place each squash in a bowl or on a plate and spoon the beef mixture into the centers. Garnish with the basil.

Nutrition:
Calories: 213
Fat: 3 g
Carbs: 9 g
Protein: 3 g
Fiber: 2.1 g
Sugar: 3 g

76. Fried Chili Beef With Cashews

Preparation time: 10 minutes
Cooking time: 25 minutes
Servings: 4
Ingredients:

- 1/2 tbsp. extra virgin olive oil or canola oil
- 1 pound sliced lean beef
- 2 tbsp. freshly squeezed lime juice
- 2 tsp. fish sauce
- 2 tsp. red curry paste
- 1 cup green capsicum, diced
- 24 cashews
- 1 tsp. arrowroot
- 1 tsp. honey
- 1/2 cup water

Directions

1. Attach oil to a pan set over medium heat; add beef and fry until its no longer pink inside. Pour in red curry paste and cook for a few more minutes.
2. Stir in honey, lime juice, fish sauce, capsicum and water; simmer for about 20 minutes.
3. Merge cooked arrowroot with water to make a paste; stir the paste into the sauce to thicken it.
4. Detach the pan from heat and add the fried cashews. Serve.

Nutrition:
Calories: 231
Fat: 12 g
Carbs: 21 g
Protein: 3 g
Fiber: 2 g
Sugar: 0.3 g

77. Coconut-Crusted Cod

Preparation time: 25 minutes
Cooking time: 10 minutes
Servings: 4
Ingredients:

- 24 ounces cod fillets, sliced into small strips
- 2 tbsp. coconut oil
- 1 cup finely shredded coconut
- 2 cups coconut milk
- 1 1/2 cups coconut flour
- 1/4 tsp. sea salt
- 1 1/2 tsp. ginger powder

Directions

1. Rinse and debone the fish fillets.
2. In a bowl, combine ginger powder, coconut flour and sea salt; set aside.
3. Add coconut milk to another bowl and set aside.
4. Add shredded coconut to another bowl and set aside.
5. Dip the fillets into coconut milk, then into the flour mixture, back into the milk, and finally into shredded coconut.
6. Add coconut oil to a skillet set over high heat; when melted and hot, add the fish fillets and cook for about 5 minutes per side or until cooked through.

Nutrition:
Calories: 212 Fat: 11 g Carbs: 19 g
Protein: 2.9 g Fiber1.5 2 g Sugar: 2.7 g

78. Curried Chicken Salad

Preparation time: 10 minutes
Cooking time: 0 minutes Servings: 3-4
Ingredients:

- 1/2 cup mashed garlic and avocado, at room temperature
- 1 tsp. apple-cider vinegar
- 1/2 lemon, juiced
- 2 tsp. powdered turmeric
- 1 tsp. powdered ginger
- 1/4 tsp. sea salt
- 1 lb. shredded pastured chicken breast
- 1/4 cup chopped red onion
- 1/4 cup raisins
- 2 tbsp. chopped parsley

Directions

1. In a bowl, merge together lemon juice, apple cider vinegar, avocado mash, ginger, turmeric and sea salt until well blended.
2. Add chicken breasts, raisins, and red onion; stir to mix well.
3. Garnish with chopped parsley and serve.

Nutrition:
Calories: 123
Fat: 12 g Carbs: 1.9 g
Protein: 2.9 g Fiber:.3 2 g
Sugar: 1.7 g

79. Mexican Chicken Served With 'Rice'

Preparation time: 10 minutes
Cooking time: 30 minutes Servings: 3
Ingredients:

- 1 pound boneless and skinless grilled chicken breast, diced into small pieces
- 1 medium avocado
- 4 tbsp. Extra virgin olive oil
- 1 can (4 ounce) diced green chilies
- 1 head cauliflower, trimmed
- 1 cup celery, finely diced
- 1 medium onion, diced
- A pinch of chili powder, ground cumin and oregano and to taste
- 1 tsp. sea salt
- Salsa, optional

Directions

1. Warmth extra virgin olive oil in a skillet set over medium heat. Add onion and sauté for about 10 minutes or until tender.
2. Add celery and sauté for 5 minutes more.
3. Process cauliflower in a food processor until you achieve the texture of rice.

4. Stir cauliflower in the onion mixture and cook, covered, for about 10 minutes or until tender.
5. Add chicken, chilies, chili powder, oregano, cumin, and sea salt.
6. Serve topped with salsa and avocado.

Nutrition:
Calories: 265 Fat: 22 g
Carbs: 11 g Protein: 2.9 g
Fiber: 3 1 g Sugar: 1.3 g

80. Asian Stir Fry

Preparation time: 45 minutes
Cooking time: 10 minutes Servings: 4
Ingredients:

- 2 tbsp. coconut oil
- 1 pound boneless, skinless chicken breast
- 1 tbsp. honey
- 2 tbsp. Vinegar
- 2 tbsp. toasted sesame oil
- 2 tbsp. arrowroot powder
- 1 cup sliced zucchini (about 1 small zucchini)
- 4 ounces stemmed and thinly sliced shiitake mushrooms (about 1 cup)
- 1 1/2 cups sliced strips of baby bock Choy
- 1 cup thinly sliced carrots
- 4 cups sliced broccoli
- 1 cup finely chopped onion
- 1/2 tsp. Sea salt
- 11/2 cups water

Directions

1. Clean and pat dry the chicken; cut into small cubes and place them on a plate.
2. Add coconut oil to a skillet set over medium heat to melt.
3. Add onion and sauté for about 10 minutes or until tender and translucent.
4. Add zucchini, mushrooms, bock Choy, and sea salt; sauté for about 5 minutes.
5. Stir in a cup of water and cook, covered, for about 10 minutes or until veggies are wilted.
6. Dissolve arrowroot powder in a bowl with 1/2 cup of water, stirring until well blended.
7. Stir the arrowroot mixture into the veggies and continue cooking for 3 minutes more or until the sauce is thick and glossy.
8. Stir in honey, sesame oil and vinegar. Serve hot.

Nutrition:
Calories: 145

Fat: 12 g Carbs: 10 g
Protein: 3 g Fiber: 4 g
Sugar: 3 g

81. Zucchini Noodles

Preparation time: 10 minutes
Cooking time: 15 minutes Servings: 2-4
Ingredients:

- 1 tbsp. extra virgin olive oil
- 1 pound zucchini
- 1 tsp. spice mix

Directions
1. Warmth extra virgin olive oil in a large sauté pan
2. Add zucchini noodles; stir in the seasoning and cook for about 5 minutes or until noodles are tender
3. Serve.

Nutrition:
Calories: 267
Fat: 10 g
Carbs: 7 g
Protein: 2 g
Fiber: 2 g
Sugar: 1 g

82. Spiced Chicken With Grilled Lime

Preparation time: 10 minutes
Cooking time: 40 minutes Servings: 4
Ingredients:

- 3 pounds bone-in chicken pieces
- 1 tbsp. garlic powder
- 1 tbsp. smoked paprika
- 2 tbsp. coconut sugar
- 6 limes, halved
- 1 tsp. allspice
- 1 tbsp. Freshly squeezed ground black pepper
- 1/2 tsp. sea salt

Directions
1. Place limes and chicken pieces in a bowl.
2. In a small bowl, mix together garlic powder, paprika, coconut sugar, allspice, pepper and salt; pour over the chicken and mix well.
3. Grill the chicken and limes over medium heat for about 20 minutes per side. Serve.

Nutrition:
Calories: 123 Fat: 9 g
Carbs: 4 g Protein: 3 g
Fiber: 1 g Sugar: 3.1 g

83. Turkey Hash

Preparation time: 10 minutes
Cooking time: 30 minutes
Servings: 4
Ingredients:

- 2 cups turkey, diced
- 3 cups pumpkin or butternut squash, skinned and sliced into small cubes
- 1 large onion, diced
- 2 tbsp. extra virgin olive oil
- 1 cup water
- 1/4 tsp. freshly ground black pepper
- 1/2 tsp. sea salt

Directions
1. Attach extra virgin olive oil to a large skillet set over medium heat; add onion and sauté for about 10 minutes, stirring, or until caramelized.
2. Add pumpkin or squash and cook, covered, for about 10 minutes
3. Add the turkey, sea salt and pepper and continue cooking for about 10 minutes.
4. Serve hot.

Nutrition:
Calories: 165
Fat: 12 g Carbs: 11 g
Protein: 2.1 g
Fiber: 3.9 g
Sugar: 2.1 g

84. Sesame Salmon Burgers

Preparation time: 25 minutes
Cooking time: 12 minutes
Servings: 12
Ingredients:

- 1 pound salmon, skin removed
- 1 tbsp. coconut flour
- 2 large free range eggs
- 1/4 cup toasted sesame seeds
- 1/4 cup finely chopped scallions (only green and white parts)
- 1 tsp. fresh ginger, peeled and minced
- 1 clove garlic, pressed
- 1 tbsp. Ume plum vinegar
- 1 tbsp. toasted sesame oil
- Coconut oil, for frying

Directions

1. Cleanse the fish and pat dry with paper towel; cut into 1/4-inch cubes.
2. Mix together eggs, sesame seeds, scallions, ginger, garlic, Ume, oil, and salmon in a large bowl.
3. Stir in the coconut flour and form small patties.
4. Add coconut oil to a skillet set over medium high heat to melt. Attach the patties and cook for about 6 minutes per side or until golden brown.
5. Place the cooked patties onto a plate lined with paper towel to serve.

Nutrition
Calories: 138 Fat: 4g
Carbs: 1g Protein: 23g
Fiber: 0g Sugar: 0g

85. Grilled Lemony Chicken

Preparation time: 6 Hours 15 Minutes
Cooking time: 10 minutes
Servings: 12
Ingredients

- 1 pound boneless and skinless chicken breasts, halved
- 1 1/2 tsp. freshly minced thyme leaves
- 1/2 tsp. freshly ground black pepper
- 1/3 cup extra virgin olive oil
- 1/3 cup lemon juice, freshly squeezed
- 1 tsp. sea salt
- 2 large carrots, julienned or grated
- 1 head Romaine lettuce, bottom chiffonier leaves removed
- Nut Sauce

Directions

1. Whip together extra virgin olive oil, lemon juice, thyme, sea salt and pepper in a bowl to make the marinade.
2. Set chicken in a baking dish; pour the marinade over the chicken and marinate in the refrigerator for at least 6 hours.
3. When ready, heat your grill and grill the chicken for about 10 minutes per side or until cooked through.
4. Detach from oven, let cool and cut into small slices.
5. To serve, place romaine on a platter and top with carrots; place the grilled chicken over the veggies and serve with the nut sauce.

Nutrition:
Calories: 17
Fat: 5 g
Carbs: 12 g
Protein: 1 g
Fiber: 3 g
Sugar: 1.3 g

86. Barbecued Salmon With Lemon And Herbs

Preparation time: 4 Hours 15 Minutes
Cooking time: 12 minutes
Servings: 12
Ingredients

- 12 (180 grams each) Atlantic salmon fillets, with skin on
- 1/2 cup extra virgin olive oil
- 1 bunch roughly chopped lemon thyme
- 1/3 cup finely chopped dill leaves
- 2 tbsp. drained and chopped capers
- 2 fresh lemons, juiced
- 2 garlic cloves, finely chopped
- A pinch of sea salt
- Lemon wedges, to garnish

Directions
1. In a large jug, mix together lemon thyme, dill, capers, 1/3 cup lemon juice, garlic, virgin olive oil, salt and pepper.
2. Set salmon fillets, in a single layer, in a ceramic dish and pour over half of the marinade. Turn it over and pour over the remaining marinade. Refrigerate, covered, for about 4 hours.
3. Detach the fish from the refrigerator at least 30 minutes before cooking.
4. Grease barbecue plate and heat on medium high. Barbecue the marinated fish, skin side down, for about 3 minutes. Turn and continue barbecuing, basting occasionally with the marinade, for 6 minutes more or until cooked through.
5. Serve garnished with lemon wedges.

Nutrition
Calories: 230
Fat: 10g Carbs: 12g

Protein: 13g
Fiber: 4g
Sugar: 0g

87. Fish With Herb Sauce

Preparation time: 15 minutes
Cooking time: 15 minutes
Servings: 4
Ingredients:

- 4 (180 grams each) white fish fillets (such as snapper or blue-eye), with skin on
- 1/3 cup extra virgin olive oil
- 1 cup roughly torn flat-leaf parsley leaves
- 3 garlic cloves, sliced
- 1 large fresh lemon
- 1/4 cup oregano leaves
- 12 basil leaves, torn
- 12 mint leaves, torn
- Crusty bread, to serve

Directions
1. Preheat your oven to 350F.
2. Peel the lemon and squeeze out the juice into a bowl; stir in extra virgin olive oil, herbs, garlic, and season. Set aside.
3. Add the remaining oil to an ovenproof pan set over medium high heat; stir in lemon rind for about 30 seconds. Set the seasoned fish in the pan, skin side down and cook for about 4 minutes or until crisp.
4. Set the pan to the oven and cook for about 5 minutes or until the fish is cooked through.
5. Detach the pan from the oven and transfer to low heat; pour over the herb mixture and cook until just warmed through. Serve with crusty bread.

Nutrition
Calories: 260
Fat: 11g
Carbs: 20g
Protein: 14g
Fiber: 12g
Sugar: 0g

88. Roasted Seafood With Herbs And Lemon

Preparation time: 15 minutes

Cooking time: 10 minutes

Servings: 4

Ingredients:

- 1/4 cup extra virgin olive oil
- 8 scallops on the half shell
- 8 large green prawns
- 8 scampi, halved and cleaned
- 2 garlic cloves, finely chopped
- 2 tbsp. chopped flat-leaf parsley
- Finely grated lemon zest
- Freshly squeezed lemon juice from 1 lemon
- 2 tbsp. finely chopped lemon thyme

Directions

1. Preheat your oven to 400F.
2. Set the seafood in a single layer in a baking dish.
3. Combine together lemon juice, zest, garlic, extra virgin olive oil, and thyme; brush over the seafood and season well.
4. Bake in the preheated oven.
5. Sprinkle with chopped parsley and serve garnished with lemon wedges.

Nutrition:

Calories: 32

Fat: 5

Fiber: 2

Carbs: 11

Protein: 4

89. Cucumber And Avocado Salad

Preparation time: 10 minutes

Cooking time: 0 minutes

Servings: 16

Ingredients:

- 1/4 cup extra virgin olive oil
- 1/4 cup lemon juice
- 175g baby salad leaves
- 2 thinly sliced Lebanese cucumbers
- 4 green onions, thinly sliced
- 2 medium avocados, chopped

Directions

1. In a bowl, combine together salad leaves, cucumber, onion, and avocado.
2. Mix together extra virgin olive oil and lemon juice in a jar and season with sea salt. Shake to merge well and pour over the salad to serve.

Nutrition:

Calories: 13 Fat: 4

Fiber: 5 Carbs: 23 Protein: 8

90. Paprika And Chili Kale Chips

Preparation time: 10 minutes
Cooking time: 12 minutes
Servings: 4
Ingredients:

- 2 tbsp. extra virgin olive oil
- 1 bunch curly kale
- 1/2 tsp. dried red chili flakes
- 1 tsp. paprika
- A pinch of sea salt

Directions

1. Preheat your oven to 350F.
2. Set two baking trays by lining them with baking papers.
3. Trim the center stems from kale and cop into small pieces.
4. In a large bowl, mix together chili, paprika, and extra virgin olive oil; add the kale and toss until well coated.
5. Spread the kale out on the prepared baking dishes and bake for about 15 minutes or until kale is crisp.
6. Sprinkle with sea salt to serve.

Nutrition:
Calories: 21
Fat: 4
Fiber: 2
Carbs: 11
Protein: 4

CHAPTER 8

Snack

91. Cinnamon And Hemp Seed Coffee Shake

Preparation Time: 5 Minutes
Cooking Time: 0 Minutes
Servings: 1
Ingredients:

- 1 1/2 frozen bananas, sliced into coins
- 1/8 teaspoon ground cinnamon
- 2 tablespoons hemp seeds
- 1 tablespoon maple syrup
- 1/4 teaspoon vanilla extract, unsweetened
- 1 cup regular coffee, cooled
- 1/4 cup almond milk, unsweetened
- 1/2 cup of ice cubes

Directions:
1. Pour milk into a blender, add vanilla, cinnamon, and hemp seeds and then pulse until smooth.
2. Add banana, pour in the coffee, and then pulse until smooth. Add ice, blend until well combined, blend in maple syrup and then serve.

Nutrition:
Calories: 410 Fat: 19.5 g Protein: 4.9 g Carbs: 60.8 g
Fiber: 6.8

92. Green Smoothie

Preparation Time: 5 Minutes
Cooking Time: 0 Minutes
Servings: 1
Ingredients:

- 1/2 cup strawberries, frozen
- 4 leaves of kale
- 1/4 of a medium banana
- 2 Medjool dates, pitted
- 1 tablespoon flax seed
- 1/4 cup pumpkin seeds, hulled
- 1 cup of water

Directions:
1. Set all the ingredients in the jar of a food processor or blender and then cover it with the lid.
2. Pulse until smooth and then serve.

Nutrition:
Calories: 204
Fat: 1.1 g;
Protein: 6.5 g;
Carbs: 48 g;
Fiber: 8.3 g

93. Strawberry And Banana Smoothie

Preparation Time: 5 Minutes
Cooking Time: 0 Minutes
Servings: 1
Ingredients:

- 1 cup sliced banana, frozen
- 2 tablespoons chia seeds
- 2 cups strawberries, frozen
- 2 teaspoons honey
- 1/4 teaspoon vanilla extract, unsweetened
- 6 ounces coconut yogurt
- 1 cup almond milk, unsweetened

Directions:
1. Set all the ingredients in the jar of a food processor or blender and then cover it with the lid.

2. Pulse until smooth and then serve.
Nutrition:
Calories: 114 Fat: 2.1 g;
Protein: 3.7 g; Carbs: 22.3 g; Fiber: 3.8 g

94. Orange Smoothie

Preparation Time: 5 Minutes
Cooking Time: 0 Minutes
Servings: 1
Ingredients:

- 1 cup slices of oranges
- 1/2 teaspoon grated ginger
- 1 cup of mango pieces
- 1 cup of coconut water
- 1 cup chopped strawberries
- 1 cup crushed ice

Directions:
1. Set all the ingredients in the jar of a food processor or blender and then cover it with the lid.
2. Pulse until smooth and then serve.
Nutrition:
Calories: 198.7 Fat: 1.2 g; Protein: 6.1 g Carbs: 34.3 g
Fiber: 0 g

95. Pumpkin Chai Smoothie

Preparation Time: 5 Minutes
Cooking Time: 0 Minutes   Servings: 1
Ingredients:

- 1 cup cooked pumpkin
- 1/4 cup pecans
- 1 frozen banana
- 1/4 teaspoon ground cinnamon
- 1/4 teaspoon cardamom
- 1/4 teaspoon ground nutmeg
- 2 teaspoons maple syrup
- 1 cup of water, cold
- 1/2 cup of ice cubes

Directions:
1. Set pecans in a small bowl, cover with water, and then let them soak for 10 minutes.
2. Drain the pecans, add them into a blender, and then add the remaining ingredients.
3. Pulse for 1 minute until smooth, and then serve.
Nutrition:
Calories: 157.5
Fat: 3.8 g   Protein: 3 g
Carbs: 32.3 g   Fiber: 4.5 g

96. Banana Shake

Preparation Time: 5 Minutes
Cooking Time: 0 Minutes
Servings: 1
Ingredients:

- 3 medium frozen bananas
- 1 tablespoon cocoa powder, unsweetened
- 1 teaspoon shredded coconut
- 1 tablespoon maple syrup
- 1 tablespoon peanut butter
- 1 teaspoon vanilla extract, unsweetened
- 2 cups of coconut water
- 1 cup of ice cubes

Directions:
1. Add banana in a food processor, add maple syrup and vanilla, pour in water and then add ice.
2. Pulse until smooth and then pour half of the smoothie into a glass.
3. Add butter and cocoa powder into the blender, pulse until smooth, and then add to the smoothie glass.
4. Sprinkle coconut over the smoothie and then serve.

Nutrition:
Calories: 301
Fat: 9.3 g;   Protein: 6.8 g
Carbs: 49 g Fiber: 1.9

97. Green Honeydew Smoothie

Preparation Time: 5 Minutes
Cooking Time: 15 Minutes
Servings: 4
Ingredients:

- 1 large banana
- 6 large leaves of basil
- 1/2 cup frozen pineapple
- 1 teaspoon lime juice
- 1 cup pieces of honeydew melon
- 1 teaspoon green tea Matcha powder
- 1/4 cup almond milk, unsweetened

Directions:
1. Set all the ingredients in the jar of a food processor or blender and then cover it with the lid.
2. Pulse until smooth and then serve.

Nutrition:
Calories: 223.5
Fat: 2.7 g   Protein: 20.1 g
Carbs: 32.7 g Fiber: 5.2 g

98. Summer Salsa

Preparation Time: 5 Minutes
Cooking Time: 15 Minutes
Servings: 8
Ingredients:

- 1 cup cherry tomatoes, chopped
- 1/4 cup chopped cilantro
- 2 tablespoons chopped red onion
- 1 teaspoon minced garlic
- 1 small jalapeno, deseeded, chopped
- 1/2 of a lime, juiced
- 1/8 teaspoon salt
- 1 tablespoon olive oil

Directions:
1. Set all the ingredients in the jar of a food processor or blender except for cilantro and then cover with its lid.
2. Pulse until smooth and then pulse in cilantro until evenly mixed.
3. Tip the salsa into a bowl and then serve with vegetable sticks.

Nutrition:
Calories: 51
Fat: 0.1 g;
Protein: 1.7 g
Carbs: 11.4 g
Fiber: 3.1 g

99. Red Salsa

Preparation Time: 35 Minutes
Cooking Time: 15 Minutes Servings: 8
Ingredients:

- 4 Roma tomatoes, halved
- 1/4 cup chopped cilantro
- 1 jalapeno pepper, deseeded, halved
- 1/2 of a medium white onion, peeled, cut into quarters
- 3 cloves of garlic, peeled
- 1/2 teaspoon salt
- 1 tablespoon brown sugar
- 1 teaspoon apple cider vinegar

Directions:
1. Switch on the oven, then set it to 425 degrees F and let it preheat.
2. Meanwhile, take a baking sheet, line it with foil, and then spread tomato, jalapeno pepper, onion, and garlic.
3. Bake the vegetables for 15 minutes until vegetables have cooked and begin to brown

and then let the vegetables cool for 3 minutes.

4. Transfer the roasted vegetables into a blender, add remaining ingredients and then pulse until smooth.

5. Tip the salsa into a medium bowl and then chill it for 30 minutes before serving with vegetable sticks.

Nutrition:

Calories: 240 Fat: 0 g Protein: 0 g Carbs: 48 g Fiber: 16 g

100. Pinto Bean Dip

Preparation Time: 5 Minutes

Cooking Time: 0 Minutes Servings: 4

Ingredients:

- 15 ounces canned pinto beans
- 1 jalapeno pepper
- 2 teaspoons ground cumin
- 3 tablespoons nutritional yeast
- 1/3 cup basil salsa

Directions:

1. Merge all the ingredients in a food processor, cover with the lid, and then pulse until smooth.

2. Tip the dip in a bowl and then serve with vegetable slices.

Nutrition: Calories: 360 Fat: 0 g Protein: 24 g Carbs: 72 g Fiber: 24 g

101. Smoky Red Pepper Hummus

Preparation Time: 5 Minutes

Cooking Time: 0 Minutes

Servings: 4

Ingredients:

- 1/4 cup roasted red peppers
- 1 cup cooked chickpeas
- 1/8 teaspoon garlic powder
- 1/2 teaspoon salt
- 1/8 teaspoon ground black pepper
- 1/4 teaspoon ground cumin
- 1/4 teaspoon red chili powder
- 1 tablespoon Tahini
- 2 tablespoons water

Directions:

Set all the ingredients in the jar of the food processor and then pulse until smooth. Tip the hummus in a bowl and then serve with vegetable slices.

Nutrition:

Calories: 489 Fat: 30 g Protein: 9 g Carbs: 15 g Fiber: 6 g

102. Spinach Dip

Preparation Time: 20 Minutes
Cooking Time: 5 Minutes
Servings: 8
Ingredients:

- 3/4 cup cashews
- 3.5ounces soft tofu
- 6 ounces of spinach leaves
- 1 medium white onion, peeled, diced
- 2 teaspoons minced garlic
- 1/2 teaspoon salt
- 3 tablespoons olive oil

Directions:

1. Set cashews in a bowl, cover with hot water, and then let them soak for 15 minutes.
2. After 15 minutes, drain the cashews and then set aside until required.
3. Take a medium skillet pan, add oil to it and then place the pan
4. Set the onion, and cook until tender, stir in garlic and then continue cooking for 30 seconds until fragrant.
5. Scoop the onion mixture into a blender, add remaining ingredients and then pulse until smooth.
6. Tip the dip into a bowl and then serve with chips.

Nutrition:
Calories: 134.6 Fat: 8.6 g
Protein: 10 g Carbs: 6.3 g
Fiber: 1.4 g

103. Tomatillo Salsa

Preparation Time: 5 Minutes
Cooking Time: 20 Minutes
Servings: 8
Ingredients:

- 5 medium tomatillos, chopped
- 3 cloves of garlic, peeled, chopped
- 3 Roma tomatoes, chopped
- 1 jalapeno, chopped
- 1/2 of a medium red onion, skinned, chopped
- 1 Anaheim chili
- 2 teaspoons salt
- 1 teaspoon ground cumin
- 1 lime, juiced
- 1/4 cup cilantro leaves
- 3/4 cup of water

Directions:

1. Take a medium pot, place it over medium heat, pour in water, and then add onion, tomatoes, tomatillo, jalapeno, and Anaheim chili.
2. Sauté the vegetables for 15 minutes, remove the pot from heat, add cilantro and lime juice and then stir in salt.
3. Remove pot from heat and then pulse by using an immersion blender until smooth.
4. Serve the salsa with chips.

Nutrition:
Calories: 317.4 Fat: 0 g
Protein: 16 g Carbs: 64 g Fiber: 16 g

104. Arugula Pesto Couscous

Preparation Time: 10 Minutes
Cooking Time: 20 Minutes Servings: 4 Ingredients:

- 8 ounces Israeli couscous
- 3 large tomatoes, chopped
- 3 cups arugula leaves
- 1/2 cup parsley leaves
- 6 cloves of garlic, peeled
- 1/2 cup walnuts
- 3/4 teaspoon salt
- 1 cup and 1 tablespoon olive oil
- 2 cups vegetable broth

Directions:

1. Take a medium saucepan, place it over medium-high heat, add 1 tablespoon oil and then let it heat.
2. Add couscous, stir until mixed, and then cook for 4 minutes until fragrant and toasted.
3. Pour in the broth, stir until mixed, bring it to a boil, switch heat to medium level and then

simmer for 12 minutes until the couscous has absorbed all the liquid and turn tender.

4. When done, remove the pan from heat, fluff it with a fork, and then set aside until required.

5. While couscous cooks, prepare the pesto, and for this, place walnuts in a blender, add garlic, and then pulse until nuts have broken.

6. Add arugula, parsley, and salt, pulse until well combined, and then blend in oil until smooth.

7. Transfer couscous to a salad bowl, add tomatoes and prepared pesto, and then toss until mixed. Serve straight away.

Nutrition:
Calories: 73 Fat: 4 g Protein: 2 g Carbs: 8 g Fiber: 2 g

105. Oatmeal And Raisin Balls

Preparation Time: 40 Minutes
Cooking Time: 0 Minutes
Servings: 4
Ingredients:

- 1 cup rolled oats
- 1/4 cup raisins
- 1/2 cup peanut butter

Directions:

1. Place oats in a large bowl, add raisins and peanut butter, and then stir until well combined.

2. Shape the mixture into twelve balls, 1 tablespoon of mixture per ball, and then arrange the balls on a sheet.

3. Set the baking sheet into the freezer for 30 minutes until firm and then serve.

Nutrition:
Calories: 135
Fat: 6 g
Protein: 8 g
Carbs: 13 g
Fiber: 4 g

106. Paleo Sweet Potato Tater Tots

Preparation Time: 5 Minutes
Cooking Time: 20 Minutes
Servings: 4

Ingredients:

- 2 Large Sweet Potatoes (Skinned and Roughly Cubed)
- 1/4 Medium Finely Diced Onion
- 2 tablespoons of Coconut Flour
- 1 teaspoon of Garlic Powder
- 1 teaspoon of Chili Powder
- 1/2 teaspoon of Salt
- 1/4 teaspoon of Freshly Ground Pepper
- 1/2 cup of Coconut Oil (For Frying)

Directions:

1. Bring your large-sized pot of water to a boil. Add your sweet potatoes and cook for approximately 5 minutes. Drain and rinse with cold water. Shake off any excess water.

2. Place your sweet potato and onion into your food processor and pulse to break down into smaller pieces. Transfer to a large-sized bowl. Stir in your coconut flour, chili powder, garlic powder, salt, and pepper. Stir well to combine.

3. With your hands to shape the potato mixture into small cylinders. Place to the side until ready to fry .Warmth your coconut oil in a heavy skillet until hot. Working in batches, add your tater tots to the skillet and fry until golden brown.

4. Serve and Enjoy!

Nutrition:
Calories: 301
Fat: 9.3 g;

Protein: 6.8 g
Carbs: 49 g
Fiber: 1.9

Paleo Cherry Pistachio
107. Granola Bars
Preparation Time: 5 Minutes
Cooking Time: 15 Minutes
Servings: 12
Ingredients:

- 2 cups of Almonds
- 1/2 cup of Pistachios (Shells Removed)
- 1/3 cup of Pepitas
- 1/4 cup of Melted Coconut Oil
- 1/2 cup of Unsweetened Coconut Flakes
- 2 tablespoons of Almond Butter
- 1/4 cup of Honey
- 1/2 cup of Chopped Dried Cherries
- 1/2 teaspoon of Vanilla Extract
- 1/2 teaspoon of Salt

Directions:
1. Preheat your oven to 325 degrees. Prepare your 8x8-inch baking pan with parchment paper. Place your almonds, pepitas, pistachios, and coconut flakes in your food processor and blend to break them down into smaller pieces.
2. Whisk together your coconut oil, vanilla, honey, almond butter, and salt in a large-sized bowl. Add in your almond mixture and dried cherries. Stir together well to evenly coat.
3. Transfer your granola to your prepared baking pan and press into a flat, even layer. Bake for approximately 25 to 30 minutes until golden brown. Allow it to cool completely. Should take approximately 1 to 2 hours. Once cooled cut it into bars. Store in your refrigerator.
4. Serve and Enjoy!

Nutrition:
Calories: 240 Fat: 0 g
Protein: 0 g Carbs: 48 g Fiber: 16 g

108. Paleo Blackberry Homemade Fruit Roll-Ups
Preparation Time: 5 Minutes
Cooking Time: 15 Minutes
Servings: 8

Ingredients:

- 1 pint of Blackberries
- 1/4 cup of Honey
- 7 Mint Leaves
- Dash of Lime Juice

Directions:
1. Preheat your oven to 170 degrees. Set your rimmed baking sheet with parchment paper. Place all of your ingredients into a blender or food processor and puree until smooth.
2. Se your mixture onto your baking sheet and spread evenly with your spatula. Bake for approximately 5 to 6 hours, or until completely dried out but still sticky.
3. Detach your pans from the oven and allow to cool for approximately 30 minutes. Cut your mixture into long strips. Set at one end and roll up each strip. Set in an airtight container.
4. Serve and Enjoy!

Nutrition:
Calories: 212
Fat: 11 g
Carbs: 19 g
Protein: 2.9 g
Fiber1.5 2 g
Sugar: 2.7 g

109. Rosemary And Thyme Baked Eggplant Fries

Preparation Time: 5 Minutes

Cooking Time: 10 Minutes

Servings: 3

Ingredients:

- 1 Medium Eggplant (Thinly Sliced)
- 1 Egg
- 1 1/2 cups of Almond Meal
- 1 teaspoon of Dried Thyme
- 1 teaspoon of Chopped Fresh Rosemary
- 1/2 teaspoon of Paprika
- 1 tablespoon of Extra-Virgin Olive Oil
- 1/2 teaspoon of Salt

Directions:

1. Preheat your oven to 450 degrees. Line your baking sheet with parchment paper. Stir together your almond meal, thyme, rosemary, salt, and paprika in a shallow dish. In a separate dish, whisk your egg and olive oil together.
2. Dip an eggplant slice into your egg mixture and then dredge in your almond flour mixture. Set on your baking sheet and repeat with your remaining eggplant. Bake for approximately 20 to 25 minutes, turning once until your fries are crispy and golden brown. Serve and Enjoy!

Nutrition: Calories: 121 Fat: 1 g Protein: 2 g Carbs: 21 g Fiber: 11 g

110. Baked Homemade Apple Cinnamon Chips

Preparation Time: 5 Minutes

Cooking Time: 20 Minutes Servings: 2

Ingredients:

- 2 Apples
- 1 teaspoon of Cinnamon

Directions:

1. Preheat your oven to 200 degrees.
2. Using your sharp knife or mandolin, slice your apples thinly. Discard the seeds.
3. Prepare your baking sheet with parchment paper and arrange your apple slices on it without overlapping. Sprinkle your cinnamon over apples.
4. Bake for approximately 1 hour, then flip. Continue baking for another 1 to 2 hours, flipping occasionally until your apple slices are no longer moist. Store in airtight container. Serve and Enjoy!

Nutrition:

Calories: 157.5 Fat: 3.8 g Protein: 3 g Carbs: 32.3 g Fiber: 4.5 g

111. Baked Homemade Beet Chips

Preparation Time: 5 Minutes

Cooking Time: 15 Minutes Servings: 4

Ingredients:

- 4 Medium Beets (Rinsed and Scrubbed)
- 2 teaspoons of Extra-Virgin Olive Oil
- 4 sprigs of Fresh Rosemary
- 4 sprigs of Fresh Thyme
- Salt
- Ground pepper

Directions:

1. Preheat your oven to 350 degrees. Peel your beets and thinly slice them. Place into a large-sized bowl and toss with your olive oil. Set to two rimmed baking sheets in a single layer. Sprinkle with pepper and salt. Chop up your rosemary and thyme and sprinkle it over your beets.
2. Bake until slightly browned. Remove from your oven and allow it to cool. Chips will become crispier as they cool.
3. Serve and Enjoy!

Nutrition:

Calories: 317.4 Fat: 0 g Protein: 16 g Carbs: 64 g Fiber: 16 g

112. Baked Homemade Sweet Potato Chips

Preparation Time: 5 Minutes
Cooking Time: 15 Minutes Servings: 4
Ingredients:

- 2 Large Sweet Potatoes
- 2 tablespoons of Melted Coconut Oil
- 2 teaspoons of Dried Rosemary
- 1 teaspoon of Sea Salt

Directions:

1. Preheat your oven to 375 degrees. Peel your sweet potatoes and slice thinly, using your mandolin or a sharp knife. In a large-sized bowl, toss your sweet potatoes with coconut oil, rosemary, and salt.
2. Place your sweet potato chips in a single layer on your rimmed baking sheet covered with parchment paper. Bake, then flip your chips over and bake for 10 more minutes. For the last ten minutes, watch your chips closely and pull off any chips that begin to brown, until all of your chips are cooked.
3. Serve and Enjoy!

Nutrition:
Calories: 32
Fat: 5
Fiber: 2
Carbs: 11
Protein: 4

113. Baked Homemade Tortilla Chips

Preparation Time: 5 Minutes
Cooking Time: 20 Minutes
Servings: 2
Ingredients:

- 1 cup of Almond Flour
- 1 Egg White
- 1/2 teaspoon of Cumin
- 1/2 teaspoon of Chili Powder
- 1/2 teaspoon of Garlic Powder
- 1/4 teaspoon of Paprika
- 1/4 teaspoon of Onion Powder
- 1/2 teaspoon of Salt

Directions:

1. Preheat your oven to 325 degrees. In a large-sized bowl, combine all of your ingredients together until they form even dough.
2. Roll out your dough between two pieces of parchment paper, as thinly as possible. Remove your top layer of parchment paper. Cut your dough into desired shapes for chips.
3. Move your dough, with the parchment paper, onto your baking sheet. Bake for approximately 11 to 13 minutes, until golden brown. Remove from your oven and allow to cool for 5 minutes. Use your spatula to remove the chips from your paper. Serve and Enjoy!

Nutrition:
Calories: 204 Fat: 1.1 g; Protein: 6.5 g; Carbs: 48 g; Fiber: 8.3 g

114. Paleo Kale Chips

Preparation Time: 5 Minutes
Cooking Time: 15 Minutes Servings: 2
Ingredients:

- 1 bunch of Kale (Washed and Dried)
- 2 tablespoons of Olive Oil
- Salt

Directions:

1. Preheat your oven to 300 degrees. Remove your center stems and either tear or cut up your leaves.
2. Toss your kale and olive oil together in a large-sized bowl; sprinkle with salt. Spread on your baking sheet (or two, depending on the amount of kale). Bake until crisp. Serve and Enjoy!

Nutrition:
Calories: 121 Fat: 1 g

Protein: 2 g Carbs: 21 g
Fiber: 11

115. Paleo Pumpkin Pie Bites

Preparation Time: 5 Minutes
Cooking Time: 15 Minutes Servings: 16
Ingredients:

- 1 cup of Pitted Medjool Dates
- 1/4 cup of Unsweetened Coconut Flakes
- 1/2 cup of Pecans
- 2 teaspoons of Vanilla
- 1/3 cup of Pumpkin Puree
- 1/4 teaspoon of Nutmeg
- 1 teaspoon of Cinnamon
- 1/4 teaspoon of Ground Cloves
- Pinch of Salt

Directions:

1. Place your dates into a small-sized bowl and cover with water. Allow to soak for approximately 10 minutes, then drain.
2. Place your pecans into your food processor and pulse until finely ground. Attach in the rest of the ingredients, including your soaked dates. Pulse until well combined. Adjust your spices to taste. Place into your refrigerator for approximately 30 minutes to chill.
3. With your hands form the dough into small-sized balls. Serve and Enjoy!

Nutrition:
Calories: 32 Fat: 3 g
Carbs: 12 g
Protein: 1 g
Fiber: 3 g Sugar: 1.9 g

116. Strawberry Homemade Fruit Leather

Preparation Time: 5 Minutes
Cooking Time: 15 Minutes
Servings: 12
Ingredients:

- 4 cups of Strawberries (Hulled and Chopped)
- 2 tablespoons of Honey

Directions:

1. Warmth your oven to 170 degrees or the lowest oven temperature setting. Line your baking sheet with parchment paper. Place your strawberries in a medium-sized saucepan and cook over a low heat until soft. Add in your honey and stir well to combine.
2. Use your immersion blender to puree your strawberries in the saucepan, or transfer to a blender and puree until smooth.
3. Pour your mixture onto the lined baking sheet and spread evenly with your spatula. Bake for approximately 6 to 7 hours, until it peels away from your parchment.
4. Once cooled, peel your fruit leather off the paper and use your scissors to cut your fruit leather into strips..
5. Serve and Enjoy!

Nutrition:
Calories: 121 Fat: 1 g Protein: 2 g Carbs: 21 g Fiber: 11 g

117. Paleo Lime Coconut Bites

Preparation Time: 5 Minutes
Cooking Time: 20 Minutes
Servings: 12
Ingredients:

- 11/2 cups of Pitted Medjool Dates
- 1/4 cup of Cashews
- 3/4 cup of Almonds
- 1/3 cup of Unsweetened Coconut Flakes
- Juice of 3 Limes
- Zest of 3 Limes
- Pinch of Salt

Directions:

1. Place your almonds and cashews into your blender or food processor and pulse to finely chop. Add your dates, salt, lime zest and juice and blend until your mixture starts to clump together.
2. Transfer to your bowl and scrape down the sides with your spatula. Use your hands to

form small-sized round balls, rolling in your palm. Roll each ball in your coconut flakes to coat.. Serve and Enjoy!

Nutrition:
Calories: 267 Fat: 10 g Carbs: 7 g Protein: 2 g
Fiber: 2 g Sugar: 1 g

118. Paleo Parsnip Fries With Truffle Oil

Preparation Time: 5 Minutes
Cooking Time: 20 Minutes
Servings: 3
Ingredients:

- 4 Medium Parsnips (Peeled)
- 2 teaspoons of Truffle Oil
- 2 tablespoons of Extra-Virgin Olive Oil
- 2 tablespoons of Chopped Parsley
- Salt - Ground pepper

Directions:

1. Preheat your oven to 400 degrees. Slice your peeled parsnips into thin fries. Toss in your bowl with the olive oil, salt, and pepper. Spread out in an even layer on your rimmed baking sheet and bake for approximately 20 minutes.
2. Turn your fries over and place back in the oven. Turn up the heat to 450 degrees. Bake for an approximately 5 to 10 minutes until crispy, watching closely to make sure that the fries do not burn.
3. Place your fries in a large-sized bowl and toss with your parsley and truffle oil.
4. Serve and Enjoy!

Nutrition:
Calories: 21 Fat: 5 g Carbs: 11 g Protein: 1 g Fiber: 5 g Sugar: 0.3 g

119. Paleo Salsa Tomato Bowls

Preparation Time: 5 Minutes
Cooking Time: 15 Minutes Servings: 4
Ingredients:

- 4 Medium Ripe Roma Tomatoes
- 1/4 cup of Finely Diced Onion
- 1/4 cup of Sliced Black Olives
- 1/2 Jalapeno (Seeded and Finely Chopped
- 1/2 Green Bell Pepper
- 1 tablespoon of Chopped Fresh Cilantro
- 2 cloves of Minced Garlic
- 2 teaspoons of Balsamic Vinegar
- 1 tablespoon of Grape seed Oil
- Salt - Pepper

Directions:

1. Cut your tomatoes in half. In a small-sized bowl, mix together your remaining ingredients. Stir together well.
2. Spoon your salsa mixture into your tomato cups. Place in the refrigerator to chill.
3. Serve and Enjoy!

Nutrition:
Calories: 157.5
Fat: 3.8 g
Protein: 3 g
Carbs: 32.3 g
Fiber: 4.5 g

120. Paleo Deviled Eggs

Preparation Time: 5 Minutes
Cooking Time: 15 Minutes
Servings: 12
Ingredients:

- 6 Eggs
- 1/4 cup of Paleo Mayonnaise
- 3 tablespoons of Finely Chopped Sun-Dried Tomatoes
- 3/4 teaspoon of Smoked Paprika
- 1/4 teaspoon of Salt
- 1 tablespoon of Chopped Fresh Cilantro

Directions:

1. Place your eggs in your saucepan and cover with cold water. Warmth on your stove and bring to a boil. Once boiling, turn off your heat and cover. Let stand for approximately 12 minutes.
2. Drain and transfer your eggs to an ice bath for a minute to cool. Peel off the shells.
3. Slice your eggs in half and scoop the yolks into a bowl. Finely mash your yolks. Stir in your mayonnaise, sun-dried tomatoes, paprika, and salt. Mix together well. Pipe into your egg white halves, top with cilantro and refrigerate.
4. Serve and Enjoy!

Nutrition:
Calories: 121
Fat: 1 g
Protein: 2 g
Carbs: 21 g
Fiber: 11 g

CHAPTER 9

Meat

121. Meatballs

Preparation time: 10 minutes
Cooking time: 20 minutes
Servings: 4
Ingredients:
- 1 pound ground beef
- 1/2 onion, chopped
- 1/2 cup chopped fresh parsley, plus 1 tablespoon for garnish
- 3 garlic cloves, finely chopped
- 1 egg, beaten
- 1/2 teaspoon dried basil
- 1/2 teaspoon dried oregano
- 1/2 teaspoon salt
- 1/2 teaspoon freshly ground black pepper
- 1 to 2 tablespoons extra-virgin olive oil

Directions:
1. In a large bowl, merge together the beef, onion, 1/2 cup of parsley, garlic, egg, basil, oregano, salt, and pepper until thoroughly merge. Using your hands, pinch off palm-size pieces of the mixture and roll into meatballs. You'll end up with 8 to 10 meatballs.
2. Set a frying pan over medium heat, heat the olive oil.

3. Gently add the meatballs to the pan, and brown on all surfaces, about 5 minutes per side.
4. Remove from the heat, garnish with the remaining 1 tablespoon of parsley, and serve.

Nutrition:
Calories 76 Fat 4.3 Fiber 0.3
Carbs 2.2 Protein 7.4

122. Burger Bowls

Preparation time: 10 minutes
Cooking time: 15 minutes
Servings: 4
Ingredients:
- 1 pound ground beef
- 1/2 onion, finely chopped, plus 1/2 onion, sliced, for topping
- 2 tablespoons homemade Ketchup (here)
- Salt
- Freshly ground black pepper
- 1 teaspoon extra-virgin olive oil
- 4 cups field greens or other lettuce
- Homemade Mayo (here), for topping
- Mustard, for topping
- Pickles, for topping
- Tomatoes, sliced, for topping

Directions:
1. In a large bowl, whip together the beef, finely chopped onion, and Ketchup until thoroughly combined. Season with salt and pepper.
2. Divide the mixture four ways and form into patties with your hands.
3. Grease a large skillet or grill pan with the olive oil, and cook the burgers.
4. Divide the field greens evenly among 4 serving bowls, and place 1 burger on top of each pile of greens. Top each burger with some onion slices, Homemade Mayo or Ketchup, mustard, pickles, sliced tomatoes, or any other toppings you prefer, and serve.

Nutrition:
Calories: 301
Fat: 9.3 g;
Protein: 6.8 g
Carbs: 49 g
Fiber: 1.9

123. Taco Salad

Preparation time: 5 minutes
Cooking time: 15 minutes
Servings: 4
Ingredients:
- 1 to 2 tablespoons extra-virgin olive oil
- 1/2 onion, diced
- 1 or 2 garlic cloves, minced
- 1 pound ground beef
- 1/4 cup cherry tomatoes (optional)
- 1 tablespoon taco seasoning
- Freshly ground black pepper
- 2 to 3 cups chopped romaine lettuce, or the salad mix of your choice
- 4 to 6 tablespoons your favorite Paleo salsa, for garnish
- 1 avocado, diced or simply quartered, for garnish
- 1 lime, cut into wedges, for garnish

Directions:
1. Set a large pan over medium heat, heat the olive oil.
2. Sauté the onion until slightly translucent, about 5 minutes. Attach the garlic, and cook for another minute.
3. Add the ground beef. Stir it around until it begins to brown, and cook all the way through, 5 to 7 minutes. If there's a lot of liquid, carefully drain it off and return the pan to the heat.
4. Add the cherry tomatoes (if using), and cook for another 2 to 3 minutes, or until they start to get wilt and some of them begin to burst. Stir in the taco seasoning, season with pepper, and remove the pan from the heat.
5. Divide the lettuce evenly among 4 bowls, and top each lettuce pile with the ground beef mixture. Garnish each salad with the salsa, avocado, and lime, and serve.

Nutrition:
Calories: 13
Fat: 9
Fiber: 12

Carbs: 21
Protein: 8

124. Hamburger And Rice-Style Ground Beef

Preparation time: 10 minutes
Cooking time: 15 minutes
Servings: 4
Ingredients:
- 1 to 2 tablespoons extra-virgin olive oil
- 4 roasted red peppers, diced
- 3 carrots, diced
- 3 garlic cloves, minced
- 1 green bell pepper, diced
- 1 onion, diced
- 11/2 pounds ground beef
- 4 tablespoons tomato paste
- 1/4 teaspoon red pepper flakes
- Salt
- Freshly ground black pepper
- 1 to 2 tablespoons sliced scallion, for garnish

Directions:
1. In a large skillet over medium heat, heat the olive oil. Sauté the red peppers, carrots, garlic, bell pepper, and onion for 5 to 7 minutes.
2. When everything is slightly browned, raise the heat to medium-high and add the ground beef. Cook until browned. Attach the tomato paste and red pepper flakes, season with salt and pepper, and stir until everything is incorporated.
3. Keep warm over low heat. Scoop into bowls, and sprinkle with the scallions.

Nutrition:
Calories 32 Fat 3.5
Fiber 0 Carbs 0.1

Protein 0

125. Shepherd's Pie

Preparation time: 10 minutes
Cooking time: 45 minutes
Servings: 4
Ingredients:
For the Filling

- 1 tablespoon extra-virgin olive oil
- 1/2 onion, grated
- 1 or 2 garlic cloves, grated
- 2 celery stalks, diced
- 2 or 3 large carrots, diced
- 1 pound ground beef
- Salt
- Freshly ground black pepper
- 2 tablespoons tomato paste
- 1 teaspoon dried mustard
- 1 teaspoon dried thyme
- 1/2 fresh rosemary sprig, chopped
- 1 cup chicken broth
- 1 cup green peas (thawed if frozen)

For the Topping

- 1 large head cauliflower, cut into florets
- 2 tablespoons grass-fed butter
- 1 teaspoon garlic powder
- Salt
- Freshly ground black pepper
- 1 to 2 tablespoons coconut milk (optional)

For Assembling the Shepherd's Pie

- 1/2 tablespoon melted butter, for brushing
- 2 tablespoons sliced scallions, for garnish

Directions:
To Make the Filling

1. Set a pan over medium heat, heat the olive oil. Sauté the onion and garlic until the onion is slightly translucent, about 5 minutes. Attach the celery and carrots, and cook for 5 more minutes.
2. Add the ground beef, and season with salt and pepper. Allow to brown, about 5 minutes, and then add the tomato paste, mustard, thyme, and rosemary. Cook until any liquid in the pan begins to evaporate.
3. Add the chicken broth, cook for 5 to 7 minutes to reduce it a bit, and then add the peas. Give it a quick stir, and transfer the mixture into one baking dish or individual ramekins.

To Make the Topping

1. While the filling is cooking, fill a large saucepan with water and bring it to a boil. Attach the cauliflower to the boiling water, and cook until it is fork-tender, about 10 minutes. Rinse the cauliflower and return to the pan.
2. Add the butter and garlic powder, and season with salt and pepper. Use a mixer or immersion blender to mash the cauliflower until it is mostly smooth. If it is too thick, add some coconut milk.

To Assemble the Shepherd's Pie

Spread the mashed cauliflower evenly over the beef, and brush the top with the additional 1/2 tablespoon of melted butter. Set under the broiler until the mashed cauliflower becomes golden-brown. Serve garnished with the scallions.

Nutrition:
Calories: 51 Fat: 0.1 g;
Protein: 1.7 g Carbs: 11.4 g Fiber: 3.1 g

126. Beef Tenderloin

Preparation time: 10 minutes
Cooking time: 35 minutes
Servings: 4-6
Ingredients:

- 1 (3-pound) beef tenderloin
- 3 tablespoons extra-virgin olive oil
- 3 garlic cloves, minced
- Salt
- Freshly ground black pepper
- 2 cups arugula, for serving

Directions:

1. Preheat the oven to 500F.
2. Remove the beef from the refrigerator about half an hour before you want to cook it, to bring it to room temperature. Place it in a roasting pan.
3. In a bowl, stir the olive oil and garlic into a paste. Season with salt and pepper. Coat the tenderloin with the garlic paste, rubbing it in well with your hands. Roast for 15 minutes, or until browned.
4. Lower the heat to 375F, and cook for another 20 minutes, or until it reaches your desired level of doneness.
5. Rest the beef for 10 to 15 minutes before slicing thinly and serving on a bed of arugula.

Nutrition:

Calories 71
Fat 4.8
Fiber 0.3
Carbs 1
Protein 6

Fat 8.1
Fiber 1.4
Carbs 11.1
Protein 3

127. Classic Pot Roast

Preparation time: 10 minutes
Cooking time: 3 hours
Servings: 4-6
Ingredients:

- 1 (3- to 4-pound) boneless chuck roast
- Salt
- Freshly ground black pepper
- 2 tablespoons extra-virgin olive oil
- 1 onion, sliced
- 2 garlic cloves, minced
- 2 celery stalks, diced
- 1/2 cup red wine (optional; omit if strict Paleo)
- 1 cup beef broth
- 2 or 3 dried bay leaves
- 2 or 3 fresh thyme sprigs
- 4 carrots, chopped
- 1 cup green peas (thawed if frozen)

Directions:

1. Preheat the oven to 350F.
2. Season the roast with salt and pepper. Dip the meat for 3 to 5 minutes per side.
3. Remove the roast from the pot, and set aside.
4. Attach the onion, garlic, and celery to the pot, and sauté until the onion is slightly translucent, about 5 minutes. Set in the wine (if using), and stir it around to deglaze the pot, scraping up any browned bits from the bottom.
5. Set the roast above of the vegetables, and add the beef broth, bay leaves, and thyme. Bring the pot into the oven, and cook.
6. Add the carrots, and cook for an additional hour. Make sure the liquid hasn't all evaporated; if it has, added a bit more.
7. Detach the pot from the oven, and add the peas. Cover the pot, and allow the peas to cook for 10 minutes while the meat rests in the dish.
8. Serve immediately.

Nutrition:
Calories 119

128. Ropa Vieja

Preparation time: 10 minutes
Cooking time: 1 hour and 20 minutes Servings: 4
Ingredients:

- 1 to 2 tablespoons extra-virgin olive oil
- 2 to 3 pounds flank steak
- 1 red onion, sliced
- 4 garlic cloves, minced
- 2 red bell peppers, cut into strips
- 2 green bell peppers, cut into strips
- 1 teaspoon dried oregano
- 1 teaspoon ground cumin
- 1/4 cup sherry vinegar
- 3 cups beef broth
- 1 tablespoon tomato paste
- 2 dried bay leaves
- Salt
- Freshly ground black pepper
- 1/2 cup chopped fresh cilantro

Directions:

1. In an oven or pot over medium-high heat, warmth the olive oil. Brown the beef (you may need to cut it in half and work in batches), about 3 minutes per side. Set aside.
2. Set the heat to medium, and attach the onion, garlic, and red and green bell peppers to the pot. Stirring frequently, cook for 5 to 7 minutes, until tender. Add the oregano and cumin, and cook for 1 minute more.
3. Attach the sherry vinegar, and deglaze the pan, stirring up any browned bits from the

bottom. Cook. Add the broth and tomato paste, and stir well to combine. Set in the bay leaves, and return the beef to the pot. Season with salt and pepper. Bring the whole thing to a simmer, reduce the heat to low, and cook for another hour.

4. Set the meat to a platter, and shred it. Serve garnished with the cilantro.

Nutrition:
Calories: 32 Fat: 5 Fiber: 2 Carbs: 11 Protein: 4

129. Vaca Frita

Preparation time: 10 minutes
Cooking time: 1 hour
Servings: 4
Ingredients:
- 2 pounds flank steak
- 1 dried bay leaf
- 2 onions, 1 quartered and the other sliced
- 2 tablespoons grass-fed butter
- 2 garlic cloves, smashed
- 1/4 cup freshly squeezed lime juice,
- 3 to 4 tablespoons extra-virgin olive oil,
- Salt
- Freshly ground black pepper

Directions:
1. In a large pot, cover the flank steak (you may need to cut it in half or even quarters), bay leaf, and quartered onion with enough water to cover the meat by an inch. Set to a boil, and then simmer over low heat for 20 minutes.
2. While the beef is cooking, in a medium skillet over medium-low heat, heat the butter. Gently cook the sliced onion until it is very soft and dark brown, about 20 minutes.
3. When the beef finishes cooking, transfer it to a platter and allow it to cool before using your hands to shred it into very thin pieces.
4. Transfer the shredded beef to a large bowl, and add the garlic and lime juice. Mix well, and then allow it to marinate for 30 minutes on the counter.
5. In a large skillet over high heat, heat 1 tablespoon of olive oil. Working in batches, fry the shredded beef in a single layer until very browned and crispy, 4 to 7 minutes per batch. Flavor with salt and pepper, and remove from the heat. Repeat with the rest of the beef, adding more oil as necessary.

6. Serve each plate of vaca frita topped with some of the sautéed onions and a wedge of fresh lime.

Nutrition:
Calories 119
Fat 8.1
Fiber 1.4
Carbs 11.1
Protein 3

130. Steak Marsala

Preparation time: 10 minutes
Cooking time: 35 minutes
Servings: 4
Ingredients:
For the Sauce
- 3 tablespoons extra-virgin olive oil
- 1/2 onion, sliced
- 10 ounces mushrooms
- 2 garlic cloves, minced
- 1/2 cup Marsala wine
- 11/2 cups beef broth
- Salt
- Freshly ground black pepper

For the Steaks
- 4 large steaks (rib eyes or sirloin)
- 4 tablespoons grass-fed butter

Directions:
To Make the Sauce
1. In a medium saucepan over medium heat, warmth the olive oil. Sauté the onion until slightly translucent, about 5 minutes. Attach the mushrooms and garlic, and cook for another 5 minutes.
2. Add the Marsala wine, and deglaze the pan, scraping up any browned bits from the bottom, and add the beef broth.
3. Flavor with salt and pepper, and cook down until the sauce begins to thicken, 8 to 10 minutes. Set the heat to low, and simmer until ready to serve.

To Cook the Steaks
1. Preheat the oven to 400F.
2. In a ovenproof skillet over high heat, sear the steaks for 2 to 3 minutes per side, until browned. Set to the oven, and cook for 6 to 10 minutes, depending on how rare you want them. Remove from the oven, and place 1 tablespoon of butter on each steak.

3. Let rest for 10 minutes before slicing. Top with the Marsala sauce, and serve.

Nutrition:

Calories: 134.6 Fat: 8.6 g

Protein: 10 g Carbs: 6.3 g Fiber: 1.4 g

131. Sausage-Stuffed-Dates Wrapped In Bacon

Preparation time: 15 minutes

Cooking time: 30 minutes

Servings: 8-10

Ingredients:

- 16 to 20 dates, pitted
- 1 pound spicy ground pork sausage
- 8 to 10 slices bacon, halved

Directions:

1. Preheat the oven to 400F.
2. Carefully slice each date down the middle
3. Make a roll of sausage in your hands. Stuff each date with a sausage oval.
4. Cover each stuffed date with half a strip of bacon, and set it on a baking sheet.
5. Bake the dates until the bacon is crispy and the sausage is cooked through, and serve.

Nutrition:

Calories: 13

Fat: 9

Fiber: 12

Carbs: 21

Protein: 8

132. Candied Bacon Salad

Preparation time: 5 minutes

Cooking time: 20 minutes

Servings: 4

Ingredients:

- 10 to 12 ounces thick-cut bacon, halved or quartered
- 1/2 cup maple syrup
- 3 to 4 cups field greens (or your favorite salad mix)
- 1/2 cup pecans
- 1/4 cup Apple Cider Vinaigrette (here)

Directions:

1. Preheat the oven to 400F.
2. On a baking sheet, set out the bacon in a single layer, and brush with the maple syrup. Bake until the bacon is as crispy. Chop or crumble the bacon into bite-size pieces.
3. In a large serving bowl, merge the greens with the pecans and Apple Cider Vinaigrette. Top with the candied bacon, and serve.

Nutrition:

Calories 32

Fat 3.5

Fiber 0

Carbs 0.1

Protein 0

133. Sesame Pork Salad

Preparation time: 30 minutes

Cooking time: 10 minutes

Servings: 4

Ingredients:

- 2 tablespoons honey
- 2 tablespoons sesame oil
- 1 tablespoon coconut aminos
- 1/2 tablespoon chili oil
- 1/2 tablespoon fish sauce
- 1/2 onion, diced
- 2 garlic cloves, minced
- 1/4 tsp. freshly ground black pepper
- 1 pound pork cutlets, cut into strips
- 2 to 3 cups chopped romaine (or your favorite salad lettuce)
- 1 or 2 tablespoons sesame seeds, for garnish

Directions:

1. In a large bowl, stir to merge the honey, sesame oil, coconut aminos, chili oil, fish sauce, onion, garlic, and pepper. Attach the pork, and marinate for at least 20 minutes.

2. Warmth a cast iron pan or skillet over high heat. Add the pork, and cook until seared on all sides, about 10 minutes.
3. Put the chopped lettuce in a large serving bowl, and top it with the cooked pork. Garnish with the sesame seeds, and serve.

Nutrition:
Calories 119
Fat 8.1
Fiber 1.4
Carbs 11.1
Protein 3

134. Ground Pork Stir-Fry

Preparation time: 5 minutes
Cooking time: 20 minutes
Servings: 4
Ingredients:
- 11/2 tablespoons extra-virgin olive oil or coconut oil
- 1/2 onion, diced
- 1 green bell pepper, cut into strips
- 10 ounces mushrooms, sliced
- 1 or 2 small zucchini, diced
- 3 garlic cloves, minced
- 1 pound ground pork
- Salt
- Freshly ground black pepper
- 1/4 teaspoon red pepper flakes

Directions:
1. Set a frying pan over medium heat, warmth the olive oil. Add the onion, and sauté until slightly translucent, about 5 minutes.
2. Add the bell pepper, mushrooms, and zucchini. Allow to cool down for another 5 minutes before adding the garlic.
3. Move all the sautéed vegetables to the outside edges of the pan, and put the ground pork in the middle. Flavor with salt and pepper, and cook, stirring with a wooden spoon to break up the pieces, until the pork and the garlic begin to brown, about 5 minutes. Stir the vegetables into the center until everything is well mixed. Set the heat up to medium-high, and cook until some of the pork begins to crisp up, about 5 minutes. Add the red pepper flakes, give it another stir, and serve hot.

Nutrition:
Calories: 204 Fat: 1.1 g;
Protein: 6.5 g; Carbs: 48 g; Fiber: 8.3 g

135. Bánh Mì Tacos

Preparation time: 1hour 15 minutes Cooking time: 10 minutes
Servings: 4
Ingredients:
For the Quick-Pickled Vegetables
- 1/4 cup white vinegar
- 1 tablespoon coconut aminos
- 1/2 cup carrots, julienned
- 1/2 cup cucumber, julienned
- 3 or 4 radishes, thinly sliced

For The Tacos
- 2 tablespoons honey
- 1 tablespoon sesame oil
- 1 teaspoon white vinegar
- 1/4 teaspoon red pepper flakes
- 1 pound pork cutlets, cut thinly into bite-size pieces
- 4 to 6 lettuce leaves, either romaine or butter lettuce
- 2 or 3 tablespoons chopped fresh cilantro, for garnish

Directions:
To Make the Quick-Pickled Vegetables
1. In a small bowl, stir to merge the vinegar with the coconut aminos. Add the carrots, cucumber, and radishes. Cover and marinate for 1 hour.

To Make the Tacos
1. In a medium bowl, stir to merge the honey, sesame oil, vinegar, and red pepper flakes. Add the pork, and stir. Marinate for 10 minutes.

2. In a skillet over medium-high heat, sauté the pork in the marinade for 5 to 7 minutes, or until the pork strips are cooked through.

3. Set up your tacos by laying out the lettuce boats and filling them with cooked pork. Top with a generous serving of the quick-pickled vegetables, and garnish with the cilantro.

Nutrition:
Calories: 32 Fat: 5 Fiber: 2 Carbs: 11 Protein: 4

136. Four-Ingredient Bacon And Spinach Frittata

Preparation time: 5 minutes
Cooking time: 25 minutes
Servings: 4
Ingredients:

- 6 slices bacon, chopped
- 10 large eggs
- 1/3 cup full-fat coconut milk or almond milk
- 4 cups baby spinach leaves
- Pinch sea salt
- Freshly ground black pepper

Directions:

1. Preheat the oven to 350F.
2. Warmth an oven-safe frying pan over medium-high heat. When the pan is hot, cook the bacon until crispy, stirring occasionally, about 7 minutes.
3. In a bowl, whip the eggs with the coconut milk and set aside.
4. When the bacon is crispy, using a spoon, remove the bacon drippings from the pan, leaving 2 tablespoons. Attach the spinach to the pan and season with salt and pepper. Cook until the spinach is wilted, about 1 minute, stirring occasionally.
5. Set the egg mixture over the bacon and spinach. Put the pan into the oven and bake for 15 to 20 minutes, until the eggs are set.
6. Remove the pan from the oven. Slice the frittata into quarters and serve.

Nutrition:
Calories 32
Fat 3.5
Fiber 0
Carbs 0.1
Protein 0

137. Open-Faced Tuna And Portobello Sandwiches

Preparation time: 10 minutes
Cooking time: 15 minutes
Servings: 2
Ingredients:

- Avocado oil for greasing pan
- 2 large Portobello mushroom caps
- 2 (5-ounce) cans tuna, drained
- 5 tablespoons Perfectly Paleo Mayonnaise or store-bought Paleo mayonnaise
- 1 tablespoon freshly squeezed lemon juice
- 1 teaspoon dried dill
- 1 teaspoon onion powder
- Pinch sea salt
- Freshly ground black pepper
- 1/4 cup sliced green olives, for serving

Directions:

1. Preheat the oven to 425F. Grease a medium oven-safe baking dish with oil.
2. Put the mushroom caps in the baking dish, gill side up. Bake for 15 minutes, until the mushroom caps are softened.
3. While the mushrooms are baking, in a medium bowl, mix the tuna, mayonnaise, lemon juice, dill, and onion powder. Season with salt and pepper.
4. When the mushroom caps are softened, remove them from the oven and place them on individual serving plates, gill-side up. Top each mushroom cap with half of the tuna mixture. Top with sliced olives and serve.

Nutrition:
Calories 119 Fat 8.1 Fiber 1.4 Carbs 11.1 Protein 3

138. Egg-Free, Nut-Free, One-Pan, 5-Ingredient

Preparation time: 10 minutes
Cooking time: 40 minutes
Servings: 4
Ingredients:

- 1/3 cup extra-virgin olive oil
- 2 tablespoons freshly squeezed lemon juice
- 1 tablespoon Italian seasoning
- 11/4 teaspoons sea salt, divided
- 1/4 teaspoon freshly ground black pepper
- 4 boneless, skinless chicken breasts
- 3 cups halved Brussels sprouts
- 1 large sweet potato
- 4 small Roma tomatoes, cut into 1/4-inch slices

Directions:

1. Preheat the oven to 400F. Set a large baking sheet with parchment paper.
2. In a large bowl, combine the olive oil, lemon juice, Italian seasoning, 1 teaspoon of sea salt, and pepper. Add the chicken breasts, Brussels sprouts, and sweet potato to the olive oil mixture and toss to coat.
3. Transfer to the baking sheet and arrange so that the chicken is evenly surrounded by the vegetables.
4. Toss the tomato slices in the remaining olive oil mixture and arrange them on top of the chicken.
5. Season the tomatoes with the remaining 1/4 teaspoon of sea salt and bake until the chicken is cooked through.

Nutrition:
Calories 119 Fat 8.1 Fiber 1.4 Carbs 11.1 Protein 3

139. Paleo Porridge

Preparation time: 10 minutes
Cooking time: 5 minutes
Servings: 4
Ingredients:

- 2 medium bananas, peeled
- 2 cups almond or coconut milk, divided
- 3/4 cup unsweetened coconut flakes
- 3/4 cup chopped pecans
- 3/4 cup chopped walnuts
- 3/4 teaspoon ground cinnamon
- Pinch sea salt
- 2 cups berries

Directions:

1. In a medium bowl, press the bananas with a fork.
2. Add 11/2 cups of almond milk, the coconut flakes, pecans, walnuts, cinnamon, and salt and stir to combine.
3. Set the mixture into a small saucepan and heat over low until warmed through, stirring continuously, about 5 minutes.
4. Gently add in the remaining 1/2 cup of almond milk, as needed, until the desired consistency is achieved.
5. Top the porridge with berries and serve hot.

Nutrition:
Calories 76
Fat 4.3
Fiber 0.3
Carbs 2.2
Protein 7.4

140. Dijon Pork Chops With Herbs

Preparation time: 5 minutes
Cooking time: 20 minutes
Servings: 3
Ingredients:

- 1 tablespoon dried thyme
- 1 teaspoon dried dill
- 1/4 teaspoon sea salt
- 1/4 teaspoon freshly ground black pepper
- 4 (4- to 6-ounce) boneless or bone-in pork loin chops, 1-inch-thick
- 1/4 cup Dijon mustard
- 2 tablespoons ghee

Directions:

1. Set a small bowl, stir together the thyme, dill, salt, and pepper. Set aside.
2. On a cutting board or plate, brush each pork chop with Dijon mustard on all sides and season with the spice mixture, pressing the spices gently into the chops with your fingers, as necessary.
3. In a large pan, dissolve the ghee over medium heat. Set the chops in the pan and cook for about 20 minutes, flipping once midway through cooking, until the outsides start to brown and the juices run clear or the internal temperature reaches 150F to 155F for medium doneness.
4. Serve the pork chops hot.

Nutrition:
Calories: 134.6 Fat: 8.6 g

Protein: 10 g Carbs: 6.3 g Fiber: 1.4 g

141. Kickin' Vinaigrette

Preparation time: 10 minutes
Cooking time: 15 minutes
Servings: 1
Ingredients:

- 3/4 cup extra-virgin olive oil
- 1/4 cup freshly squeezed lemon juice
- 1 jalapeño pepper, seeded and finely chopped
- 1 garlic clove, finely chopped
- 1 tablespoon finely chopped fresh mint
- 1 teaspoon finely chopped fresh oregano
- 1/2 teaspoon sea salt

Directions:

In a bowl or a blender, whisk the olive oil, lemon juice, jalapeño, garlic, mint, oregano, and salt.

Nutrition:
Calories 119 Fat 8.1
Fiber 1.4 Carbs 11.1 Protein 3

142. Parchment Pouch Salmon With Cauliflower Rice

Preparation time: 15 minutes Cooking time: 15 minutes
Servings: 4
Ingredients:

- 11/2 pounds salmon, cut into 4 pieces
- 2 tablespoons extra-virgin olive oil
- Pinch sea salt
- Freshly ground black pepper
- 1 small head cauliflower, or 4 cups cauliflower rice
- 1 teaspoon dried parsley

- 4 lemons, cut into 1/4-inch-thick slices

Directions:

1. Preheat the oven to 375F.
2. Using a pair of scissors, cut four pieces of parchment paper into 121/2-by-16-inch rectangles and set them aside.
3. Set the salmon on a plate, brush with olive oil, and then season with sea salt and pepper. Set aside.
4. Set the cauliflower into florets and place in a food processor. Pulse several times until cauliflower resembles grains of rice. Alternatively, finely dice florets by hand. In a bowl, toss the cauliflower rice with the parsley.
5. Arrange a sheet of parchment on the counter so that the short sides are to your left and right and the long sides are at the top and bottom. Transfer 1 cup of the cauliflower rice to the middle of a sheet of parchment. Next, place one piece of the salmon on top of the cauliflower rice. Lay three or four slices of lemon over the salmon.
6. Set the sides of the parchment up around the cauliflower rice and salmon and fold the top ends over two or three times. Then fold the sides over several times, crimping the paper to form a closed pouch. Repeat with remaining cauliflower and salmon and place all four pouches side by side on a large rimmed baking sheet. Reserve any remaining lemon slices for garnish.
7. Bake for 15 minutes for medium or 20 minutes for well-done salmon..

Nutrition:
Calories: 51 Fat: 0.1 g;
 Protein: 1.7 g Carbs: 11.4 g Fiber: 3.1 g

143. Rosemary Lamb Burgers

Preparation time: 5 minutes
Cooking time: 10 minutes
 Servings: 4
Ingredients:

- 1 pound ground lamb
- 1 tablespoon finely chopped fresh rosemary or 11/2 teaspoons dried rosemary
- 1/2 teaspoon sea salt
- 1/4 teaspoon freshly ground black pepper
- 1 tablespoon avocado oil, ghee, or coconut oil
- 4 large lettuce leaves, for serving

Directions:

1. In a medium bowl, merge the ground lamb, rosemary, salt, and pepper and use your hands to mix together. Form the lamb mixture into four patties.
2. Set a large skillet, heat the oil over medium heat and add the burgers. Cook the burgers, flipping as needed until done, about 5 minutes per side.
3. To serve, wrap each burger in a lettuce leaf.

Nutrition:

Calories 71

Fat 4.8

Fiber 0.3

Carbs 1

Protein 6

144. Paleo Tzatziki Sauce

Preparation time: 10 minutes

Cooking time: 15 minutes

Servings: 1 1/2 cups

Ingredients:

- 1/2 cup full-fat coconut milk
- 1/2 cup Perfectly Paleo Mayonnaise or store-bought Paleo mayonnaise
- 1 medium cucumber, finely chopped
- 1 tablespoon freshly squeezed lemon juice
- 1 tablespoon chopped fresh dill
- 1 teaspoon minced garlic
- Pinch sea salt
- Pinch freshly ground black pepper

Directions:

1. In a medium bowl, merge the coconut milk, mayonnaise, cucumber, lemon juice, dill, garlic, salt, and pepper and mix together until thoroughly combined.

Nutrition:

Calories 119 Fat 8.1 Fiber 1.4 Carbs 11.1 Protein 3

145. Anti-Inflammatory Lemon-Turmeric Smoothies

Preparation time: 5 minutes

Cooking time: 15 minutes

Servings: 2

Ingredients:

- 1 cup full-fat coconut milk
- 1 cup ice
- 1/4 cup collagen powder
- 1 medium banana, peeled
- 1 medium lemon, juiced
- 1 teaspoon ground turmeric
- Pinch freshly ground black pepper

Directions:

In a blender, combine the coconut milk, ice, collagen powder, banana, lemon juice, turmeric, and pepper and process until smooth. Serve immediately.

Nutrition:

Calories: 13

Fat: 9

Fiber: 12

Carbs: 21

Protein: 8

146. Stir-Fry Steak And Crisp Greens Salad

Preparation time: 10 minutes
Cooking time: 10 minutes
Servings: 4
Ingredients:

- 1 large head romaine lettuce, chopped (12 cups chopped romaine)
- 11/2 pounds flank steak
- 1 tablespoon avocado oil, ghee, or coconut oil
- 1 small yellow onion, thinly sliced
- 1 tablespoon coconut aminos
- 1 teaspoon sea salt
- 1/2 teaspoon freshly ground black pepper
- 2 medium red bell peppers, sliced
- 1 cup green beans
- 1 tablespoon extra-virgin olive oil
- 1 tablespoon balsamic vinegar

Directions:

1. Put the chopped lettuce in a large bowl and set aside.
2. On a cutting board, slice the steak across the grain into 1/4-inch strips and then set the strips in half so they are 4 inches long or less. Set aside.
3. Set a large skillet, heat the oil over medium heat. Sauté the onions for 2 minutes, until they start to turn translucent.
4. Increase the heat to medium-high and add the beef, coconut aminos, salt, and pepper. Fry the beef until it starts to brown but is still red in the center and then attach the bell peppers and green beans. Cook until the green beans turn a bright color and the beef is cooked to your liking.
5. Using tongs or a slotted spoon, transfers the contents of the stir-fry to the bowl of lettuce. Set with olive oil and balsamic vinegar and toss all the ingredients together. Serve on individual plates.

Nutrition:
Calories 169
Fat 16.1
Fiber 2.8
Carbs 4.4
Protein 4

147. Turkey And Veggie Stir-Fry Breakfast

Preparation time: 5 minutes
Cooking time: 10 minutes
Servings: 4
Ingredients:

- 3 tablespoons avocado oil, ghee, or coconut oil, divided
- 12 ounces ground turkey
- 1 teaspoon sea salt
- 1 small onion
- 1 bell pepper, any color, cut into 1-inch chunks
- 2 cups Swiss chard, cut into 2-inch strips
- 1/2 cup loosely chopped fresh mixed herbs, such as basil and parsley

Directions:

1. In a pan, heat 1 tablespoon of oil over medium heat. Add the ground turkey and salt. Cook the turkey, stirring occasionally, until no longer pink, about 5 minutes. Remove the turkey from the pan and set aside, leaving any excess fat in the pan.
2. Sauté the onion and bell pepper until the pepper softens and the onion begins to turn translucent, adding the additional 2 teaspoons of oil, if needed, to prevent scorching.
3. Attach the ground turkey back into the pan, along with the chard and herbs, and stir. Serve immediately.

Nutrition:
Calories 119 Fat 8.1 Fiber 1.4 Carbs 11.1 Protein 3

148. Savory Sausage Stew

Preparation time: 20 minutes
Cooking time: 40 minutes   Servings: 4
Ingredients:

- 1 tablespoon avocado oil, ghee, or coconut oil
- 1 pound mild Italian sausage
- 1 small butternut squash, cut into 1/2-inch chunks
- 2 large carrots, cut into 1/4-inch rounds
- 3 medium celery stalks
- 1 medium onion, chopped
- 3 garlic cloves, minced
- 2 teaspoons dried thyme
- 4 cups Gut-Healing Bone Broth or store-bought chicken broth

- 1 (15-ounce) can fire-roasted diced tomatoes
- 1/2 cup water
- 1 teaspoon sea salt
- 1/2 teaspoon freshly ground black pepper
- 1/4 teaspoon ground cumin
- 2 cups chopped spinach

Directions:
1. In a large pot, warmth the oil over medium heat. Add the sausage, breaking it up into chunky pieces and stirring occasionally with a wooden spoon for about 6 minutes, or until browned.
2. Add the squash, carrots, celery, onion, garlic, and thyme. Cook and turn a bright color. Set the heat to high and add the broth, diced tomatoes and their juices, water, salt, pepper, and cumin.
3. When the stew starts to boil, reduce the heat to low, cover the pot, and simmer for 30 minutes.
4. Stir in the spinach just before serving.

Nutrition:
Calories: 204
Fat: 1.1 g;
Protein: 6.5 g;
Carbs: 48 g;
Fiber: 8.3 g

149. Lacinato Kale Salad With Ham And Salami

Preparation time: 5 minutes
Cooking time: 10 minutes
Servings: 2
Ingredients:
- 4 cups stemmed and chopped lacinato kale
- 4 ounces salami, cut into bite-size pieces
- 4 ounces ham, cut into bite-size pieces
- 2 medium tomatoes, chopped
- 1/4 cup chopped pepperoncini peppers
- 2 tablespoons extra-virgin olive oil
- 1 tablespoon balsamic vinegar
- Pinch sea salt
- Pinch freshly ground black pepper

Directions:
1. In a large bowl, combine the kale, salami, ham, tomatoes, and pepperoncini peppers. Set aside.
2. In a small bowl, merge together the olive oil, balsamic vinegar, salt, and pepper.
3. Add the dressing to the kale mixture and toss to coat everything completely. Divide the salad onto plates and serve.

Nutrition:
Calories 76 Fat 4.3 Fiber 0.3 Carbs 2.2 Protein 7.4

150. Carnitas

Preparation time: 10 minutes
Cooking time: 1 hour 30 minutes
Servings: 4
Ingredients:
- 2 tablespoons extra-virgin olive oil
- 1 (2-pound) pork shoulder
- Salt
- Freshly ground black pepper
- 3 to 4 cups water
- 4 garlic cloves, crushed
- 3 fresh thyme sprigs
- 2 dried bay leaves
- 2 teaspoons dried oregano

Directions:
1. Preheat the oven to 325F.
2. Set an ovenproof pot or Dutch oven heat, heat the olive oil. Season the pork shoulder with salt and pepper, and gently lower it into the pot. Sear on each side until browned. Add the water, garlic, thyme, bay leaves, and oregano, and transfer the pot to the oven.
3. Cook the pork through and can easily be shredded with a couple of forks. Shred the whole thing, stir it around in the cooking liquid, and serve.

Nutrition:
Calories 119
Fat 8.1
Fiber 1.4
Carbs 11.1
Protein 3

CHAPTER 10

Poultry

151. Paleo Pizza Chicken

Preparation time: 10 minutes Cooking time: 30 minutes Servings: 4
Ingredients:
- 1 tablespoon pizza seasoning
- 2 teaspoons salt
- 1-2 tablespoon extra-virgin olive oil
- 24-30 slices uncured pepperoni
- 1/2 cup pizza sauce, sugar free
- 8 chicken thighs

Directions
1. Set the oven to around 425 degrees F and then put chicken thighs in a pan, preferably a 13x9.
2. Remove the skin from each chicken meat and then add 1 to 2 tablespoons of the sauce on the thighs.
3. Top each of the thighs with 4 to 5 slices of the pepperoni, before pulling the skin back on so that you cover the sauce and pepperoni.
4. Now drizzle the oil on the thigh and season with pizza seasoning and some salt.
5. Bake the meat until the skin is browned, or for about 40 to 50 minutes.

Nutrition:
Calories 119
Fat 8.1
Fiber 1.4
Carbs 11.1
Protein 3

152. Lebanese Lemon Chicken

Preparation time: 10 minutes
Cooking time: 30 minutes
Servings: 6-9
Ingredients:
- 2 sprigs of fresh thyme
- 2 sprigs of fresh rosemary
- 2 large shallots or 1 large onion
- 3 pounds boneless, skinless chicken thighs
- Black pepper, freshly ground
- 11/2 teaspoons flaky sea salt
- 1/2 teaspoon ground turmeric
- 2 tablespoons extra virgin olive oil
- 3 lemons

Directions
1. Obtain 2 tablespoons of lemon juice then set the juice in a large bowl along with black pepper, sea salt and turmeric.
2. Attach chicken to the bowl and toss to blend with the seasonings. Allow the thighs to marinate for a few minutes.
3. Then proceed to cut off the ends of 2 lemons before slicing them into rounds of 1/4 inch thick.
4. Next, half and peel the shallots, then discard the seeds before slicing the deseeded shallots.
5. Over medium-high heat, warm two large cast irons then add olive oil so that it coats the bottom. Divide the thighs between two pans with the skin side of the chicken facing own.
6. Cook the chicken thighs.
7. At this point, set the meat to a plate using slotted spatula or a pair of tongs. Then add in herb sprigs, shallots and the lemons to the pan.

8. Allow the ingredients to cook for 3 to 4 minutes or until the lemons are brown. Now pour half cup of water into every pan and stir as you scrap the browned bits from the pan.

9. Set the heat to medium, and then add in the meat to the pans. Cook until the flavors meld, in about 4 to 5 minutes.

10. You can now serve the lemon chicken with pan juices and shallots over cauliflower rice.

Nutrition:
Calories 169
Fat 16.1
Fiber 2.8
Carbs 4.4
Protein 4

153. Chicken With Fig And Shallot Compote

Preparation time: 10 minutes
Cooking time: 30 minutes
Servings: 4-6
Ingredients:
- 1 pint figs, finely chopped
- 3 shallots, halved and thinly sliced
- 1 lemon
- Black pepper, freshly ground
- 2 teaspoons ghee
- 1 teaspoon flaky sea salt
- 8 bone-in, skin-on chicken thighs

Directions
1. Heat the oven to 450 degrees F. Meanwhile, season all sides of the chicken with salt.
2. Heat a large skillet and then add oil or ghee to the hot pan. Set the bottom of the pan with oil then add in the chicken, with the skin side facing down.
3. Season the chicken with pepper and cook over medium-high heat until the chicken is deep golden brown, or for about 10 minutes.
4. Once done, turn off the heat, flip over the meat and then season the skin side using pepper.
5. Set the skillet to the oven and roast until the chicken is cooked through, or for around 20 to 25 minutes.
6. As the chicken roasts, zest the lemon to make thin strips before you juice it to obtain about 2 tablespoons of juice.
7. Now remove the roasted chicken from the oven and move the meat from the skillet to a plate. Cover using a foil to cool down.

8. Set off all the fat from the skillet reserving only a tablespoon. Over medium-high heat, add half of the lemon zest and the shallots to the pan.
9. Cook the mixture.
10. Set the heat to medium then add in the figs to the pan. Cook the mixture for about 2 to 3 minutes or until the figs are heated through; while stirring frequently.
11. At this point, merge in a tablespoon of lemon juice and taste the dish. Adjust the seasonings i.e. lemon juice, salt and pepper.
12. Serve the meat hot with warm compote drizzled on top. You can garnish with lemon wedges or lemon zest if you like.

Nutrition:
Calories 32 Fat 3.5 Fiber 0 Carbs 0.1 Protein 0

154. Grilled Chicken Satay

Preparation time: 5 minutes
Cooking time: 30 minutes
Servings: 2
Ingredients:
For Chicken
- Skewers
- 2 chicken breasts, boneless, skinless; 1 inch chunks

For Sauce
- 1/2 teaspoons red pepper flakes
- 2 garlic cloves chopped
- 1 teaspoons ginger, freshly ground
- 2 tablespoons coconut aminos
- 1 lime or 2 tablespoons lime juice
- 1 cup coconut milk
- 1/2 cup sunflower seed butter

Directions

1. In a food processor, set the ingredients for sauce and then combine until smooth to the consistency of a smoothie mixture.
2. Scoop about a 1/3 of the sauce to marinate the chicken chunks or the whole chicken in the fridge for about 3 hours to 48 hours.
3. Once prepared to cook the chicken, continue to preheat your grill for around 10 minutes and then turn down heat to medium i.e. 450-500 degrees F.
4. Slam the chicken using the skewers while on the grill and continue to cook for 6 minutes on each of the sides until it's done.
5. You can serve with a of cauliflower couscous garnished with pineapple or with freshly sautéed vegetables.

Nutrition:
Calories 76
Fat 4.3 Fiber 0.3
Carbs 2.2
Protein 7.4

155. Green Chile Chicken Breasts With Sauce

Preparation time: 5 minutes
Cooking time: 30 minutes
Servings: 6
Ingredients:

- 1 tablespoon sesame seeds, toasted
- 2 tablespoons whipping cream
- 1 tablespoon canola oil
- 6 chicken breast cutlets or fillets
- 3/4 teaspoon of salt, divided
- 1 clove garlic, thinly sliced
- 3 tablespoons slivered almonds, toasted
- 3 scallions, sliced, separated white and green parts
- 3/4 cup of fresh green chilies, chopped and seeded
- 1/2 cup chicken broth, reduced-sodium
- 2 cups almond milk, unsweetened

Directions

1. In a medium-sized saucepan, mix together green chilies, almond milk, garlic, scallion whites, broth and 1/4 teaspoon salt and bring the mixture to a boil.
2. Then minimize the heat and simmer for about 20-30 minutes, until the mixture is reduced by half.

3. Now set the mixture in a blender or immersion blender until smooth.
4. Using the remaining 1/2 teaspoon of salt, season the chicken and then heat some oil over medium-heat in a large non-skillet.
5. In the skillet, cook half of the chicken for about 1-2 minutes each side, until browned.
6. Then put the first batch of the chicken in the pan and then pour the sauce. Cook at low heat to simmer, for about 4-7 minutes until the chicken is tender and cooked through.
7. When done, remove from heat and then pour the sauce over your chicken.
8. Use the reserved sesame seeds and scallion greens to sprinkle on top. Serve and enjoy.

Nutrition:
Calories 169 Fat 16.1
Fiber 2.8 Carbs 4.4 Protein 4

156. Turkey Breast With Maple Mustard Glaze

Preparation time: 10 minutes
Cooking time: 30 minutes
Servings: 4-6
Ingredients:

- 1 tablespoon of ghee
- 2 tablespoons Dijon mustard
- 1/4 cup maple syrup
- 1/2 teaspoon black pepper, freshly ground
- 1 teaspoon salt
- 1/2 teaspoon smoked paprika
- 1/2 teaspoon dried sage
- 1 teaspoon dried thyme
- 5-pound whole turkey breast
- 2 teaspoons olive oil

Directions

1. To begin with, preheat your Air fryer to 350F.
2. Then brush olive oil over the turkey breast to coat it.
3. Combine pepper, salt, paprika, sage and thyme and then rub the seasonings on the turkey breast.
4. Place the seasoned turkey breast to the basket of Air fryer and cook for 25 minutes on the pre-heated oven.
5. Flip over the breast and then fry the other side for about 12 minutes. Check whether the internal temperature has reached 165F, which means the meat is fully cooked.

6. Meanwhile, mix together ghee, mustard and maple syrup in a small saucepan. After the turkey breast is cooked, turn it to an upright position and brush graze all over.

7. Then air fry for another 5 minutes until the skin is brown and crispy. Allow the turkey breast to cool when loosely covered with foil for about 5-10 minutes then slice and serve.

Nutrition:

Calories 119

Fat 8.1

Fiber 1.4

Carbs 11.1

Protein 3

157. Chicken Soup

Preparation time: 10 minutes

Cooking time: 1 hour 30 minutes

Servings: 4-6

Ingredients:

- 1700ml water
- 4 chicken drum sticks
- 2 celery stalks
- 1-2 carrots
- 1 onion
- 1 tablespoon salt
- Pinch pepper

Directions:

1. Pre-heat a saucepan over medium heat, add water.
2. Wash the vegetables and dry them with paper towels.
3. Chop the ends of carrots and celery stalks. Skin the onion.
4. Put all the ingredients into the saucepan, cover with the lid and simmer for 90 minutes stirring from time to time.

5. As the soup is ready, separate the chicken meat from bones and add to the soup.
6. Pour the soup in the bowls.

Nutrition:

Calories 76

Fat 4.3

Fiber 0.3

Carbs 2.2

Protein 7.4

158. Chicken Mustard Stew

Preparation time: 5 minutes

Cooking time: 1 hour 15 minutes

Servings: 6

Ingredients:

- 1 chicken
- 120ml white wine
- 2 onions
- 6 garlic cloves
- 1 can chopped tomatoes
- 2 bay leaves
- 5-6 tablespoons mustard
- 2 tablespoons cooking fat
- 1 tablespoon herbs de Provence
- Pinch salt and pepper

Directions:

1. Butcher the chicken into breasts, drums, thighs and wings, cut them into small pieces.
2. Warmth the pot over medium heat; add cooking fat and fry chicken pieces for 20 minutes till they are brown.
3. Slice onion, mince garlic cloves.
4. Warmth the saucepan over medium heat, add cooking fat, put onion and garlic, cook for 5 minutes.
5. Pour white wine, add chopped tomatoes, herbs de Provence, salt and pepper to the saucepan. Stir occasionally, bring to a boil and simmer for 10 minutes.
6. Add cooked chicken pieces to the saucepan and cook for 45 minutes.
7. Add mustard, stir thoroughly and transfer the stew to the bowls.

Nutrition:

Calories 119

Fat 8.1

Fiber 1.4

Carbs 11.1

Protein 3

159. Baked Chicken Legs

Preparation time: 5 minutes
Cooking time: 55 minutes Servings: 3
Ingredients:

- 6 chicken legs, skin-on
- 2 tablespoons coconut oil
- 1/4 tablespoon onion powder
- 1/4 tablespoon garlic powder
- 1/4 tablespoon turmeric
- 1/4 tablespoon cinnamon
- 1/4 tablespoon cumin
- 1/4 tablespoon oregano
- 1/4 teaspoon black pepper

Directions:

1. Pre-heat an oven over medium heat, cover the baking dish with the parchment.
2. Place chicken legs on the parchment, grease them with coconut oil
3. Mix spices and spread the mixture over the chicken.
4. Bake the chicken for 45-50 minutes.

Nutrition:
Calories: 204 Fat: 1.1 g; Protein: 6.5 g; Carbs: 48 g; Fiber: 8.3 g

160. Greek-Style Lamb Kabobs

Preparation time: 5 minutes
Cooking time: 15 minutes
Servings: 2-4
Ingredients:

- 1 lb. lamb stew meat;
- 1 bell pepper;
- 2 zucchini;
- 1 red onion;
- Juice of 2 lemons;
- 1/2 tsp. dried oregano;
- 1/2 tsp. sea salt;
- 1/2 tsp. black pepper;
- 1/4 cup extra-virgin olive oil;

Directions:

1. Cut meat in cubes and cut pepper, zucchini, and onion into 1-inch pieces.
2. Warmth an outdoor or indoor grill to medium-high heat.
3. Alternate meat cubes with vegetables on heat-safe skewers.
4. Mix the lemon juice with the spices in a mixing bowl.
5. Brush the sauce over the skewers and set aside for 10 minutes.
6. Put the skewers onto the grill.
7. Cook for 3-4 minutes on each side.
8. Drizzle with oil before serving.

Nutrition:
Calories 32
Fat 3.5
Fiber 0
Carbs 0.1
Protein 0

161. Grilled Whole Trouts

Preparation time: 10 minutes
Cooking time: 30 minutes
Servings: 2
Ingredients:

- 2 medium trouts;
- butter;
- 1 bunch fresh dill;
- 1 bunch fresh flat leaves parsley;
- 2 lemons;
- sea salt and black pepper;

Directions:

1. Scale, gutter and clean the trouts.
2. Slash the fishes about 8 times on each side with a knife.
3. Rub the fish with butter and add sea salt and black pepper to taste.
4. Slice one lemon and halve the other one.
5. Set the cavity with herbs and lemon slices.
6. Place the fish on a frying dish.
7. Sprinkle the lemon zest on the trouts and add some butter.
8. Place the fish in the oven, closer to the top
9. Cook for 6 minutes per side.
10. Drizzle with juice of roasted lemon.

Nutrition:
Calories 76
Fat 4.3

Fiber 0.3
Carbs 2.2
Protein 7.4

162. Moroccan Chicken

Preparation time: 10 minutes
Cooking time: 15 minutes
Servings: 4
Ingredients:
- 1 kg chicken fillets
- 1 orange
- 1 lemon
- 1 chili
- 2 garlic cloves
- 1 tablespoon cooking fat
- 1 tablespoon olive oil
- 4 tablespoons pine nuts
- 4 tablespoons chopped mint
- 1 teaspoon chili flakes
- 2 teaspoon cinnamon
- 3 teaspoon cumin
- Pinch salt and pepper

Directions:
1. Wash fruit, wipe them with paper towels. Slice orange, squeeze juice from lemon.
2. Chop chili and garlic cloves, pour lemon juice and olive oil, add chili flakes, cinnamon, cumin, pine nuts, salt and pepper. Mix.
3. Cut chicken fillets into strips, coat them in the mixture and put in the fridge for 30 minutes.
4. Warmth a pan over medium heat, add cooking fat.
5. Place the strips on the pan, fry for 2 minutes on one side, toss and add sliced orange. Cook for 2 more minutes.
6. Add chopped mint, stir thoroughly and transfer to the plates

Nutrition:
Calories 169
Fat 16.1
Fiber 2.8
Carbs 4.4
Protein 4.6

163. Grilled Chicken, Tomato And Avocado Stack

Preparation time: 10 minutes
Cooking time: 30 minutes
Servings: 4
Ingredients:
- 2 chicken breast halves (about 0,25 lb.), boneless and skinless;
- 2 large beefsteak tomatoes;
- 3 tbsp. mayonnaise;
- 1 large avocado;
- 1/4 red onion;
- 1 tbsp. olive oil;
- Any lettuce;
- Sea salt to taste;
- Freshly ground black pepper to taste;
- Fresh herbs for garnish;

Directions:
1. Season chicken breasts with salt and pepper. Slice tomatoes and onion.
2. Slice avocado into 8 thin pieces.
3. Warmth olive oil in a pan, add chicken and cook for 4 minutes per side at medium heat. Remove from the heat and let cool.
4. Line the bottom of each plate with lettuce.
5. Add a little mayonnaise in the middle, while making the stack.
6. Alternate all the ingredients and add onion slices on top.
7. Drizzle with olive oil, garnish with fresh herbs and serve.

Nutrition:
Calories 169 Fat 16.1 Fiber 2.8 Carbs 4.4
Protein 4

164. Italian Chicken Casserole

Preparation time: 10 minutes
Cooking time: 30 minutes
Servings: 4-6
Ingredients:

- 1 lb. cut chicken;
- 1 yellow onion;
- 1/4 cup coconut/olive oil;
- 3 garlic cloves;
- 1/2 cup dry white wine
- 1 tbsp. arrowroot flour;
- 1 can diced tomatoes;
- 1 bay leaf;
- 1 tsp. dried marjoram;
- 1 1/2 tsp. sea salt;
- 1 tsp. freshly ground black pepper;

Directions:

1. Preheat oven to 350 degrees.
2. Slice garlic and thinly slice onion.
3. Sprinkle chicken with salt and pepper.
4. Add oil to a large oven proof pan over medium heat.
5. Brown chicken on all sides. Cover and cook. Remove chicken to a large baking dish.
6. Leave 2 tablespoons of drippings, add onion and garlic and saute until tender.
7. Combine flour and 1/4 cup wine and stir well. Pour in the pan, add liquid and tomatoes.
8. Cook for 2 minutes, stirring occasionally.
9. Add bay leaf, thyme, marjoram and pepper, then the chicken back and cover with mushrooms, olives, celery and carrots. Pour in 1/4 cup of wine. Bring to a boil, cover, cook in the oven for 20 minutes, add cappers and bake for more 15 minutes. Serve warm.

Nutrition:
Calories 169
Fat 16.1
Fiber 2.8
Carbs 4.4

Protein 4

165. Bacon And Chicken Salad

Preparation time: 5 minutes
Cooking time: 30 minutes
Servings: 4
Ingredients:

- 1 chicken breast
- 8 rashers bacon
- 500ml water
- 5 tomatoes
- 1/2 lemon
- 1/2 avocado
- 50g rocket leaves
- 2 tablespoons olive oil
- 2 tablespoons balsamic vinegar

Directions:

1. Pre-heat a large saucepan over medium heat, pour water.
2. Squeeze juice from lemon into the water, bring to a boil.
3. Add chicken, cover with the lid and simmer for 15-20 minutes. Remove from heat and leave to cool.
4. Warmth a frying pan over high heat, add 1 tablespoon olive oil.
5. Cut rashers bacon into strips, remove the fat and put in the frying pan. Cook for 2-3 minutes and remove from the pan.
6. Cut tomatoes into quarters, transfer to the pan when bacon is removed, and fry for 2 minutes.
7. Dice cooled breast and avocado, put in the bowl. Add fried tomatoes, bacon, rocket leaves. Pour the remaining oil and vinegar, mix thoroughly.

Nutrition:
Calories 169   Fat 16.1   Fiber 2.8
Carbs 4.4   Protein 4

CHAPTER 11

Fish And Sea Foods

166. Lemon-Butter Tilapia

Preparation time: 5 minutes
Cooking time: 15 minutes
Servings: 2
Ingredients:

- 2 tablespoons grass-fed butter
- 1 garlic clove, sliced
- 2 (6-ounce) tilapia fillets
- Salt
- Freshly ground black pepper
- 1/2 lemon, plus 2 lemon slices for garnish
- 2 tablespoons chopped fresh parsley, for garnish

Directions:

1. In a medium pan over low heat, dissolve the butter. attach the garlic, and simmer for about 5 minutes.
2. Flavor both sides of the fish with a sprinkle of salt and pepper. Set the fillets in the pan, and cook on one side. Press the half lemon over the fish.
3. Angle the pan to gather the butter, and spoon it over the fish. Repeat a few times, and detach the pan from the heat.
4. Set the fish with a slice of lemon.

Nutrition:
Calories 32
Fat 3.5 Fiber 0
Carbs 0.1 Protein 0

167. Ceviche

Preparation time: 6 hours and 10 minutes
Cooking time: 10 minutes
Servings: 4
Ingredients:

- 1 pound halibut, diced
- Juice of 2 large lemons
- Juice of 4 limes
- 1/2 red onion, thinly sliced, divided
- 1 garlic clove, minced
- 1 jalapeño pepper, thinly sliced
- Salt
- Freshly ground black pepper
- 1 or 2 tablespoons sliced scallion, for garnish

Directions:

1. In a large glass bowl, cover the diced fish with the lemon juice and lime juice. Stir, and add half the onion. Cover and refrigerate until the fish is completely opaque. Stir halfway through the marinating time to make sure the citrus is evenly "cooking" the fish.
2. Remove the fish from the refrigerator, drain, and discard the marinade. In a clean bowl, stir to combine the fish with the remaining onion, the garlic, and the jalapeño. Season with salt and pepper.
3. Spoon into serving dishes, top with the sliced scallion, and serve.

Nutrition:
Calories 60 Fat 2.3
Fiber 0.8 Carbs 5.7 Protein 5.6

168. Sesame Marinated Fish

Preparation time: 25 minutes
Cooking time: 10 minutes
Servings: 5
Ingredients:

- 1 tablespoon sesame oil
- 1 tablespoon fresh ginger, minced
- 1 teaspoon garlic, minced
- 1 teaspoon coconut aminos
- 1 teaspoon ground fresh chili paste
- 4 white fish fillets
- Freshly ground black pepper
- 1 to 2 tablespoons sliced
- scallions, for garnish

Directions:

1. In a small bowl, stir to merge the sesame oil, ginger, garlic, coconut aminos, and chili paste. Using a brush spread the marinade onto the fish. Marinate in the refrigerator for 20 minutes.
2. Detach the fish from the marinade (discard the marinade, although you can spoon a couple of tablespoons over the fish while it's cooking, if you like). Set a large skillet over medium-high heat, cook the fish for about 5 minutes on each side, or until it turns white and begins to get flaky. Season with pepper.
3. Garnish with scallions and serve hot.

Nutrition:
Calories 169
Fat 16.1
Fiber 2.8
Carbs 4.4
Protein 4.6

169. Baked Tilapia

Preparation time: 5 minutes
Cooking time: 20 minutes
Servings: 4
Ingredients:

- 4 (6-ounce) pieces tilapia
- Salt
- Freshly ground black pepper
- 1/2 to 1 tablespoon garlic powder
- 1/4 teaspoon red pepper flakes
- 4 tablespoons grass-fed butter
- Juice of 1 lemon
- 1/4 cup chopped fresh parsley

Directions:

1. Preheat the oven to 400F.
2. In an 8-by-12-inch baking dish, season the pieces of fish with salt, pepper, garlic powder, and red pepper flakes. Top with 1 tablespoon of butter on each piece of fish.
3. Bake for 15 minutes, or until the fish is white and opaque throughout.
4. Detach from the oven, and pour the lemon juice over the fish. Serve with a lemon and a parsley.

Nutrition
Calories: 321
Fat: 11 g
Carbs: 5 g
Protein: 21 g
Fiber: 3.5 g
Sugar: 1 g

170. Fish Cakes

Preparation time: 15 minutes
Cooking time: 10 minutes
Servings: 4
Ingredients:
For The Fish Cakes

- 2 (6-ounce) fillets white fish
- 2 tablespoons almond flour
- 1 large shallot, minced
- 1/4 cup Homemade Mayo (here)
- Zest of 1 lemon
- Juice of 1/2 lemon
- 1/4 cup minced fresh parsley
- 2 tablespoons Dijon mustard
- 1 large egg, slightly beaten
- 1 teaspoon ground paprika
- Salt
- Freshly ground black pepper
- 2 tablespoons extra-virgin olive oil

For The Chili Sauce

- 2 tablespoons hot chili oil
- 1/4 cup apple cider vinegar
- 1/4 cup olive oil

To Serve

- 1/2 cup mizuna (or other lettuce)
- 1/2 cup arugula
- 1 carrot, julienned
- 1 small red Chile, sliced

Directions:

1. Chop the fish into a fine mince, and place in a large bowl.
2. Add the almond flour, shallot, Homemade Mayo, lemon zest and juice, parsley, mustard, egg, paprika, salt, and pepper, and mix well. Shape the mixture into four large cakes or eight smaller ones (smaller will be easier to turn over when cooking).
3. Set a large nonstick sauté pan over medium-high heat, heat the olive oil. Add the fish cakes, and allow them to brown, 4 to 5 minutes. Gently flip each one, reshaping as needed, and brown the other side, 4 to 5 minutes more.

For the chili sauce, combine all ingredients in a small bowl.

4. To serve, layer greens, carrot, and chills on serving plates, and top with fish cakes and chili sauce as desired.

Nutrition
Calories: 230 Fat: 10g Carbs: 12g Protein: 13g Fiber: 4g Sugar: 0g

171. Citrus-Baked Fish

Preparation time: 10 minutes
Cooking time: 15 minutes
Servings: 4
Ingredients:

- Ingredients: 2 lemons, sliced, divided
- 3 limes, sliced, divided
- 4 to 6 (6-ounce) fillets white fish (such as cod)
- Salt
- Freshly ground black pepper
- 1 tablespoon chopped fresh dill
- 1 tablespoon chopped fresh parsley

Directions:

1. Preheat the oven to 400F.
2. Set an 8-by-12-inch baking dish, layer half of the sliced lemons and limes to cover the bottom of the pan. Set with the fish fillets, and season with salt and pepper.
3. Layer the remaining lemon and lime slices on top, and bake for 10 to 15 minutes.
4. Remove from the oven, and serve the fish topped with the dill and parsley.

Nutrition Calories: 170 Fat: 10g Carbs: 2g Protein: 22g Fiber: 0g Sugar: 0g

172.Poached Fish With Vegetables

Preparation time: 10 minutes
Cooking time: 15 minutes
Servings: 2
Ingredients:

- 2 tablespoons grass-fed butter
- 2 (6-ounce) pieces white fish (such as cod or halibut)
- 1/2 cup diced onion
- 1/4 cup diced carrot
- 1/4 cup diced celery
- 2 or 3 fresh thyme sprigs, plus an extra pinch for garnish
- 1 large rosemary sprig, plus an extra pinch for garnish
- 2 or 3 fresh sage leaves (or pinch dried)
- 1 cup vegetable broth
- Salt
- Freshly ground black pepper

Directions:

1. In a skillet over medium-high heat, melt the butter.
2. Quickly sear the fish, about 1 minute on each side. Detach it from the pan, and add the onion, carrot, celery, thyme, rosemary, and sage to the pan. Stir and sauté for 5 minutes.
3. Pour the vegetable broth into the skillet, and bring to a simmer. Return the fish to the skillet, and slowly poach until cooked throughout, 5 to 7 minutes.
4. Flavor with salt and pepper, and serve garnished with more fresh herbs.

Nutrition:
Calories: 32
Fat: 5
Fiber: 2
Carbs: 11
Protein: 4

173.Mahi Mahi With Mango-Peach Salsa

Preparation time: 15 minutes
Cooking time: 10 minutes
Servings: 4
Ingredients:
For The Mango-Peach Salsa

- 1 avocado, diced
- 1 mango, diced
- 1 peach, diced
- 1/2 pineapple, diced
- 1/2 red onion, minced
- Juice of 1 lime
- 1 bunch fresh cilantro, chopped
- 1/4 teaspoon ground cayenne pepper

For The Fish

- 4 (6-ounce) pieces mahi mahi
- 1 to 2 tablespoons extra-virgin olive oil
- Salt
- Freshly ground black pepper
- Chopped fresh cilantro, for garnish
- 1 or 2 limes, quartered

Directions:
To Make the Mango-Peach Salsa

1. In a large bowl, mix the avocado, mango, peach, pineapple, red onion, lime juice, cilantro, and cayenne. Set with plastic wrap, and refrigerate until ready to serve.

To Make the Fish

1. Preheat the grill to medium-high.
2. Set the fish with the olive oil, and flavor with salt and pepper. Grill per side, until the fish is opaque all the way through.
3. Serve the fish hot with a couple of tablespoons of the salsa on top or on the side. Garnish with extra cilantro and a wedge of lime.

Nutrition:
Calories: 23
Fat: 11
Fiber: 12
Carbs: 25
Protein: 9

174. Fish Stew

Preparation time: 5 minutes
Cooking time: 25 minutes
Servings: 4
Ingredients:

- 5 shallots, sliced
- 4 slices bacon, diced
- 3 garlic cloves, minced
- 1/2 cup white wine (optional; omit if strict Paleo)
- 11/2 cups chicken broth
- 1 (28-ounce) can crushed tomatoes
- 20 small scallops
- 12 ounces white fish (such as haddock)
- Salt
- Freshly ground black pepper

Directions:

1. In a saucepan over medium heat, sauté the shallots, bacon, and garlic for 7 to 10 minutes, until the bacon is crisp.
2. Pour in the wine or a splash of the chicken broth, and deglaze the pan,.
3. Attach the broth and tomatoes to the pot, and cook for another 5 minutes.
4. Gently add the scallops and fish, and cook for 5 to 10 minutes more, or until all the seafood is opaque and cooked through.
5. Season with salt and pepper, and serve.

Nutrition:
Calories 169
Fat 16.1   Fiber 2.8
Carbs 4.4 Protein 4.6

175. Sea Bass Topped With Crab

Preparation time: 5 minutes
Cooking time: 10 minutes
Servings: 4
Ingredients:

- 1 tablespoon extra-virgin olive oil
- 4 (6-ounce) pieces sea bass
- 8 ounces crab meat, drained
- 1 tablespoon freshly squeezed lemon juice
- 1 teaspoon chopped fresh thyme leaves
- Salt
- Freshly ground black pepper
- 1 or 2 tablespoons sliced scallion, for garnish

Directions:

1. In a large skillet over medium-high, warmth the olive oil. Fry the sea bass. Cook for an additional 3 minutes on the other side.
2. In a small bowl, merge the crab meat with the lemon juice and thyme. Season with salt and pepper.
3. Plate the fish, and serve topped with the crab meat and garnished with the sliced scallions.

Nutrition:
Calories 60 Fat 2.3
Fiber 0.8 Carbs 5 Protein 5.6

176. Balsamic Vinaigrette

Preparation time: 5 minutes
Cooking time: 0 minutes
Servings: 4
Ingredients:

- 1 cup extra-virgin olive oil
- 1/2 cup balsamic vinegar
- 1 garlic clove, minced
- 1 tablespoon Dijon mustard
- Pinch salt
- Pinch freshly ground black pepper

Directions:

1. In a jar with a firmly fitting lid, shake or mix well to combine the olive oil, vinegar, garlic, Dijon mustard, salt, and pepper.
2. Store refrigerated, and takes it out 20 minutes before using, since the dressing will need time to come to room temperature.

Nutrition:
Calories: 204
Fat: 1.1 g;
Protein: 6.5 g;
Carbs: 48 g;
Fiber: 8.3 g

177. Bacon-Wrapped Shrimp

Preparation time: 10 minutes
Cooking time: 10 minutes
Servings: 4
Ingredients:

- 1 pound shrimp, peeled and deveined (you can leave the tails on)
- 12 slices bacon, halved, plus more if necessary
- Chopped fresh parsley, for garnish

Directions:

1. Preheat the oven to 400F.
2. Wrap a piece of bacon around each shrimp, and line them up on a baking sheet. Bake for 8 to 10 minutes, or until the bacon is crispy.
3. Detach from the oven and serve hot on a platter, sprinkled with parsley.

Nutrition:
Calories 32
Fat 3.5   Fiber 0
Carbs 0.1   Protein 0

178. Blackened Shrimp Tacos

Preparation time: 10 minutes
Cooking time: 10 minutes
Servings: 4
Ingredients:

- 11/2 pounds shrimp, peeled and deveined
- 2 tablespoons extra-virgin olive oil, divided
- 2 to 3 tablespoons Blackening Spice Mix (here)
- 8 lettuce cups, either romaine leaves or butter lettuce
- 4 tablespoons salsa
- 1 avocado, cut into slices
- 1 lime, cut into wedges

- 3 to 4 tablespoons chopped fresh cilantro, for garnish

Directions:

1. In a large bowl, drizzle the shrimp with 1 tablespoon of olive oil, and add the Blackening Spice Mix. Use your hands to thoroughly mix until all the shrimp are coated with seasoning.
2. In a large pan over medium heat, heat the remaining 1 tablespoon of olive oil. Add the shrimp, and stir quickly until pink, 5 to 7 minutes.
3. Serve the shrimp in the lettuce cups, topped with the salsa, sliced avocado, and a wedge of lime and garnished with the cilantro.

Nutrition:
Calories 71
Fat 4.8
Fiber 0.3
Carbs 1
Protein 6

179. Thai Shrimp Salad

Preparation time: 10 minutes
Cooking time: 0 minutes
Servings: 4
Ingredients:

- 2 garlic cloves, minced
- 2 or 3 scallions, chopped
- 1/4 cup freshly squeezed lime juice
- 2 cups chopped romaine lettuce
- 11/2 pounds cooked, chilled shrimp, peeled and deveined
- 1/2 red onion, thinly sliced
- 1/4 cup cherry tomatoes, chopped
- 1 large cucumber, julienned
- 5 to 10 fresh mint leaves, chopped
- 1 small bunch fresh cilantro, chopped

Directions:

1. In a small bowl, merge the garlic, scallions, lime juice, fish sauce, and chili powder, and season with salt and pepper.
2. In a large bowl, set the chopped romaine and shrimp. Add the onion, tomatoes, and cucumber. Pour the dressing over the salad, and toss well. Top with the mint and cilantro, and serve immediately.

Nutrition
Calories: 321
Fat: 11 g

Carbs: 5 g
Protein: 21 g
Fiber: 3.5 g
Sugar: 1 g

180. Shrimp Salad With Tomato And Lemon

Preparation time: 10 minutes
Cooking time: 0 minutes
Servings: 4
Ingredients:

- 11/2 to 2 pounds cooked shrimp, chilled
- 10 ounces cherry tomatoes, at room temperature (don't refrigerate at all)
- 2 garlic cloves, minced
- 1/2 red onion, thinly sliced
- Juice of 2 lemons
- 2 tablespoons extra-virgin olive oil
- Salt
- Freshly ground black pepper
- 1/4 cup fresh parsley, chopped

Directions:

1. In a large bowl, mix well to combine the shrimp, tomatoes, garlic, red onion, lemon juice, and olive oil. Season with salt and pepper.

2. Serve right away, topped with the fresh parsley.

Nutrition
Calories: 230
Fat: 10g
Carbs: 12g
Protein: 13g
Fiber: 4g
Sugar: 0g

CHAPTER 12

Dessert

181. Paleo Mayo

Preparation time: 10 minutes
Cooking time: 0 minutes Servings: 10
Ingredients:

- 1 cup sesame oil
- 1 egg
- 1/4 teaspoon salt
- 1 tablespoon lemon juice
- 1 teaspoon mustard

Directions:

1. Crack the egg in the mason jar.
2. Add sesame oil, lemon juice, salt, and mustard.
3. With the help of the immersion blender blend the mixture until you get the smooth white sauce.

Nutrition:
Calories 201
Fat 22.3
Fiber 0.1
Carbs 0.2
Protein 0.6

182. Spicy Ketchup

Preparation time: 10 minutes
Cooking time: 15 minutes
Servings: 2
Ingredients:

- 1/2 cup tomatoes, chopped
- 1/4 teaspoon chili flakes
- 1/4 teaspoon salt
- 1/4 teaspoon raw honey
- 1 teaspoon Italian seasonings
- 1 tablespoon coconut flour

Directions:

1. Put tomatoes in the saucepan.
2. Add chili flakes, salt, and Italian seasonings.
3. Bring the tomatoes to boil and then blend them with the help of the immersion blender until you get the smooth liquid.

4. Add honey and coconut flour and whisk the mixture to get rid of lumps.
5. Simmer the ketchup for 10 minutes on the medium heat.
6. Then pour the cooked ketchup in the glass jar and let it cool.

Nutrition:
Calories 33 Fat 1.3
Fiber 1.8, Carbs 4.8,
Protein 0.9

183. Salmon Pickle Boats

Preparation time: 15 minutes
Cooking time: 0 minutes
Servings: 6
Ingredients:

- 3 pickled cucumbers
- 1 egg, hard-boiled, peeled
- 4 oz. salmon, canned
- 1 teaspoon coconut cream
- 1/2 teaspoon minced garlic

Directions:

1. Cut the pickled cucumbers into halves.
2. Then remove the cucumber meat to get the shape of boats.
3. Mix up cucumber meat, canned salmon, coconut cream, and minced garlic in the mixing bowl.

4. Then chop the eggs and add them in the salmon mixture too.
5. Stir the mixture well.
6. Fill the pickled cucumber boats with salmon mixture.

Nutrition:
Calories 60 Fat 2.3 Fiber 0.8 Carbs 5.7
Protein 5.6

184. Sweet Potato Fries

Preparation time: 10 minutes
Cooking time: 18 minutes Servings: 4
Ingredients:
- 2 sweet potatoes
- 1 tablespoon sunflower oil
- 1/2 teaspoon dried basil
- 1/4 teaspoon salt

Directions:
1. Skin the sweet potatoes and divide them into the French fries.
2. Then sprinkle the sweet potato fries with dried basil, salt, and sunflower oil.
3. Preheat the oven to 360F.
4. Set the baking tray with baking paper and put the sweet potato fries in it.
5. Flatten them in one layer and transfer in the oven. Bake until they are light brown.

Nutrition:
Calories 32 Fat 3.5 Fiber 0 Carbs 0.1 Protein 0

185. Kale Chips With Almond Parmesan

Preparation time: 10 minutes
Cooking time: 20 minutes Servings: 6
Ingredients:
- 1pound kale, roughly chopped
- 2 oz. nut Parmesan, grated
- 1/2 teaspoon salt
- 1 tablespoon sunflower oil

Directions:
1. Put the chopped kale in the big bowl and sprinkle with salt and sunflower oil.
2. Then add nut Parmesan and shale the kale well.
3. After this, preheat the oven to 375F.
4. Set the baking tray with baking paper and put kale inside.
5. Flatten it well and transfer in the oven.
6. Bake the chips for 20 minutes. Shake them every 3 minutes to avoid burning.

Nutrition:
Calories 113 Fat 7.1 Fiber 2.3 Carbs 9.9 Protein 4.3

186. Hard-Boiled Eggs With Chili Flakes

Preparation time: 10 minutes
Cooking time: 7 minutes
Servings: 2
Ingredients:
- 2 eggs
- 1 teaspoon chili flakes
- 1 teaspoon mustard
- 1 cup of water

Directions:
1. Pour water in the pan and add eggs.
2. Boil them for 7 minutes and then cool under cold water.
3. After this, peel the eggs and cut into halves.
4. Then remove the egg yolks and put them in the bowl.
5. Add mustard and chili flakes.
6. Churn the mixture until smooth.
7. After this, fill the egg whites with mustard egg yolks.

Nutrition:
Calories 71 Fat 4.8
Fiber 0.3 Carbs 1
Protein 6

187. Carrot Fries

Preparation time: 10 minutes
Cooking time: 10 minutes
Servings: 4
Ingredients:
- 2 carrots, peeled
- 1 tablespoon coconut oil
- 1 teaspoon dried dill

Directions:
1. Cut the carrots on the French fries and sprinkle with dill.
2. Then put the coconut oil in the skillet and melt it.

3. Put the carrots fries in the skillet in one layer and roast for 3 minutes from each side on the medium heat.
4. Then dry the cooked fries with the help of the paper towel.

Nutrition:
Calories 42
Fat 3.4
Fiber 0.8
Carbs 3.1
Protein 0.3

188. Roasted Nut Mix

Preparation time: 10 minutes
Cooking time: 10 minutes
Servings: 6
Ingredients:

- 3 pecans, chopped
- 1/2 cup almonds, chopped
- 1/4 cup walnuts, chopped
- 1/2 cup hazelnuts, chopped
- 1 tablespoon avocado oil
- 1 teaspoon salt

Directions:
1. Heat up the avocado oil in the skillet and add chopped pecans, almonds, walnuts, and hazelnuts.
2. Add salt and mix up the mixture.
3. Roast it for 10 minutes on the medium heat. Stir the nut mix frequently.

Nutrition:
Calories 169
Fat 16.1
Fiber 2.8
Carbs 4.4
Protein 4.6

189. Raspberry And Apple Fruit Leather

Preparation time: 10 minutes
Cooking time: 45 minutes
Servings: 6
Ingredients:

- 1 cup raspberries
- 1/2 cup apple, chopped

Directions:
1. Preheat the oven to 345F.
2. Line the baking tray with baking paper.
3. After this, put the raspberries and apples in the blender and blend until you get a smooth mixture.
4. Pour it in the baking tray and flatten well.
5. Bake the mixture for 45 minutes or until it is dry.
6. Then cut it into strips and roll into rolls.

Nutrition
Calories 20
Fat 0.2
Fiber 1.8
Carbs 5
Protein 0.3

190. Baked Apple With Hazelnuts

Preparation time: 15 minutes
Cooking time: 20 minutes
Servings: 8
Ingredients:

- 4 Granny Smith apples
- 4 teaspoons almond butter
- 2 tablespoons raw honey
- 2 oz. hazelnuts, chopped

Directions:

1. Cut the apples into halves and remove seeds.
2. Then make the medium size holes in the apple halves and fill them with almond butter, raw honey, and hazelnuts.
3. Place the apples in the tray and bake for 20 minutes at 350F.

Nutrition:
Calories 167
Fat 9
Fiber 4.2
Carbs 22.4
Protein 3.1

191. Banana Mini Muffins

Preparation time: 10 minutes
Cooking time: 10 minutes
Servings: 2
Ingredients:

- 2 eggs, beaten
- 1 banana, peeled
- 1/4 teaspoon ground cinnamon

Directions:

1. Mash the banana with the help of the fork until it is smooth.
2. Then add ground cinnamon and eggs. Stir the mixture well.
3. Pour the egg-banana mixture in the non-sticky muffin molds and bake at 365F for 10 minutes.

Nutrition:
Calories 116
Fat 4.6
Fiber 1.7
Carbs 14.1
Protein 6.2

192. Nuts And Raisins Apple Rings

Preparation time: 15 minutes
Cooking time: 0 minutes
Servings: 5
Ingredients:

- 2 big apples
- 2 tablespoons raisins
- 2 tablespoons hazelnuts, chopped
- 1 tablespoon almond butter

Directions:

1. Core the apples and slice them.
2. Then mix up together raisins and hazelnuts.
3. Spread the apple slices with almond butter and sprinkle with hazelnut mixture.

Nutrition:
Calories 89 Fat 3.1
Fiber 2.8 Carbs 16.1 Protein 1.3

193. Chocolate Energy Balls

Preparation time: 15 minutes
Cooking time: 0 minutes
Servings: 5
Ingredients:

- 4 dates, chopped
- 3 oz. cashew, chopped
- 1 tablespoon cocoa powder

Directions:

1. Set the dates in the blender and blend until you get a smooth mixture.
2. Then add cashew and cocoa powder.
3. Blend mixture for 30 seconds more.
4. Then remove it from the blender and make 5 energy balls with the help of the fingertips.

Nutrition:
Calories 119 Fat 8.1
Fiber 1.4 Carbs 11.1
Protein 3

194. Turkey Sticks

Preparation time: 15 minutes
Cooking time: 10 minutes
Servings: 4
Ingredients:

- 6 oz. turkey breast, skinless, boneless
- 1 teaspoon tomato paste
- 1/2 teaspoon ground turmeric
- 1 tablespoon olive oil
- 1/2 teaspoon lemon juice

Directions:

1. Cut the turkey breast on medium-size sticks (strips).
2. Then mix up together tomato paste and olive oil.
3. Add lemon juice and ground turmeric.
4. After this, mix up turkey sticks and oil mixture.
5. Preheat the skillet until it is hot.
6. Put the turkey sticks in the skillet in one layer and roast them for 5 minutes from each side or until they turkey sticks are a little bit crunchy.

Nutrition:
Calories 76
Fat 4.3
Fiber 0.3
Carbs 2.2
Protein 7.4

195. Veggie Sticks

Preparation time: 10 minutes
Cooking time: 0 minutes
Servings: 4
Ingredients:

- 1 red sweet pepper
- 2 celery stalks
- 1 carrot, peeled
- 1 teaspoon coconut cream
- 1/4 teaspoon tahini paste

Directions:

1. Cut the sweet pepper, celery stalk, and carrot into the sticks.
2. Then put them in the plate side-by-side and sprinkle with coconut cream and tahini paste.

Nutrition:
Calories 22 Fat 0.6
Fiber 1 Carbs 4.1
Protein 0.6

196. Fresh Fruit Salad

Preparation time: 15 minutes
Cooking time: 15 minutes
Servings: 5
Ingredients:

- Apples
- Oranges
- Grapes
- Raspberries
- Bananas
- Kiwi Fruit
- Watermelon
- Cantaloupe
- Blackberries
- Blueberries

Directions:

1. Simply place a combination of any of the above washed, chopped fresh fruits in a decorative serving bowl for a delicious dessert. Sprinkle with blanched almonds for a treat. Too easy!

Nutrition:
Calories 167
Fat 9
Fiber 4.2
Carbs 22.4
Protein 3.1

197. Berry Paleo Ice Cream

Preparation time: 15 minutes
Cooking time: 15 minutes
Servings: 5
Ingredients:

- 1 can coconut milk (370g, full fat)
- 2 cups of fresh or frozen berries, (thawed if frozen)
- 1 tsp. vanilla bean (extract)
- 1/4 cup raw honey

Directions:

1. Set aside 1/4 of the berries. Place the rest into blender and puree. Add coconut milk, honey and vanilla; blending on high for approx. 1 minute.
2. Tip remaining berries into the mix and just stir.
3. Pour mixture into an electric ice cream maker and until frozen, thick and creamy. Serve with some extra berries on the side!

Nutrition:
Calories 32
Fat 3.5
Fiber 0
Carbs 0.1
Protein 0

198. Apple Cider Donuts

Preparation time: 15 minutes
Cooking time: 10 minutes
Servings: 4
Ingredients:

- 1/2 cup coconut flour
- 1/2 cup apple cider
- 2 eggs
- 4 Tbsp. coconut oil
- 2 Tbsp. raw honey
- 1/2 tsp. cinnamon
- 1/2 tsp. baking soda
- pinch of salt

For cinnamon sugar:

- 1/2 cup coconut sugar
- 1 Tbsp. cinnamon

Directions:

1. Preheat donut maker (can also use a mini-donut maker).
2. In a small bowl merge together all the dry ingredients: coconut flour, 1/2 teaspoon of cinnamon and salt.
3. In a bigger bowl combine eggs, 2 tablespoons of coconut oil and honey.
4. Attach the dry ingredients to the wet ones and whisk them together until the dough is smooth.
5. Mix in the apple cider and stir well.
6. Scoop the dough into the donut maker. Cook for 3 minutes.
7. Mix together coconut sugar with 1 tablespoon cinnamon.
8. Remove the donuts from the donut maker and let them cool down a bit.
9. Brush each donut with the remaining coconut oil, and then toss them in the coconut sugar and cinnamon mixture.

Nutrition:
Calories 76 Fat 4.3
Fiber 0.3 Carbs 2.2 Protein 7.4

199. Coconut Milk Ice Cream

Preparation time: 15 minutes
Cooking time: 15 minutes
Servings: 5
Ingredients:

- 2 (13-oz.) cans of chilled coconut milk or cream
- 1 3/4 cups raw organic sugar
- 2 tsp. vanilla extract
- 1 Tbsp. shredded coconut (optional)

Directions:

1. Empty the cans of coconut milk into your blender.
2. Add the sugar and the vanilla. Blend until air bubbles rise. Taste test for sugar and vanilla.
3. Now add the shredded coconut.
4. Place into a freezer safe container. If you own an ice cream maker, set the mixture in, then add shredded coconut last.
5. Freeze for 1/2 an hour.
6. Set it out of the freezer and whisk it briskly or churn using a blender to get air back into the mix.
7. Return to the freezer.
8. Repeat until your ice cream is creamy and frozen.

Nutrition:
Calories 71
Fat 4.8
Fiber 0.3
Carbs 1
Protein 6

200. Crepe With Fresh Fruits

Preparation time: 15 minutes
Cooking time: 15 minutes
Servings: 6
Ingredients:

- 2 Tbsp. coconut flour
- 3 free range eggs
- 1 tsp. raw honey
- 1/2 cup coconut milk
- 1 Tbsp. vanilla extract
- Fresh fruit
- Cinnamon

Directions:

1. Mix flour, coconut milk, eggs, honey and vanilla.
2. Heat a non-stick fry pan greased with olive oil on med heat. Pour 1/4 cup of mixture into fry pan; cooking till edges are light brown then flip to cook other side.
3. Repeat till batter is all gone; keeping crepes warm.
4. Fill each crepe with fresh fruit with some spilling out onto plate for decoration.
5. Sprinkle lightly with cinnamon. You may also like to pour on some maple syrup. *Makes about 6 crepes

Nutrition:
Calories 119 Fat 8.1 Fiber 1.4 Carbs 11.1
Protein 3

201. Super Easy Chocolate Mousse

Preparation time: 15 minutes
Cooking time: 15 minutes
Servings: 8
Ingredients:
- 3 large dates, de seeded (fresh or dried)
- 1 soft avocado
- 1 banana
- 1 Tbsp. of good quality carob or cacao powder (from health store)
- 1/2 tsp. vanilla extract

Directions:
1. Blend up really well, like a smoothie and place in a glass or bowl to chill.
2. Top with fresh strawberries of other fruit you have on hand. Healthy too with the good fats, protein, vitamin b and potassium.

Nutrition:
Calories 169 Fat 16.1
Fiber 2.8 Carbs 4.4
Protein 4.6

202. Dark Chocolate Coconut Pudding

Preparation time: 15 minutes
Cooking time: 15 minutes
Servings: 6
Ingredients:
- 2 cups full fat coconut milk
- 3.5oz (100g) dark natural chocolate, chopped into small pieces
- 4 sheets of natural gelatin
- 1/2 tsp. vanilla extract

Directions:
1. Dip the gelatin sheets in cold water for five minutes.
2. Meanwhile heat the coconut milk on low heat. You don't need it to boil, just get it warm enough for gelatin to dissolve.
3. When the coconut milk is very warm, take it off the heat and stir in the dark chocolate pieces until they melt. Add vanilla extract.
4. Discard the water where the gelatin sheets were soaking. Add the softened gelatin sheets to the coconut milk and stir until they dissolve.
5. Pour the chocolate pudding in cups.
6. Let the chocolate pudding cool for few hours before serving. Decorate with strawberries and enjoy!

Nutrition:
Calories: 21Fat: 5 g
Carbs: 11 g Protein: 1 g
Fiber: 5 g Sugar: 0.3 g

203. Easy Strawberry Ice Cream

Preparation time: 15 minutes
Cooking time: 15 minutes
Servings: 6
Ingredients:
- 1lb (450g) strawberries, greens removed
- 14 oz. (400ml) coconut milk
- 1/2 Tbsp. lemon juice
- stevia extract to taste

Directions:
1. Place all ingredients in the food processor. Blend until smooth.
2. Freeze. The ice cream will be very hard when frozen because there is no sugar, so take it out before serving to let it soften a bit.
3. Serve with fresh sliced strawberries or other berries and coconut cream.

Nutrition:
Calories: 51 Fat: 0.1 g; Protein: 1.7 g
Carbs: 11.4 g Fiber: 3.1 g

204. Beet Chocolate Pudding

Preparation time: 15 minutes
Cooking time: 20 minutes
Servings: 4
Ingredients:

- 1/8 teaspoon sea salt
- 1/2 teaspoon of cinnamon, ground
- 1/3 cup pure maple syrup
- 1/2 cup canned coconut milk
- 1/2 cup red beet roasted
- 1/2 cup of unsweetened cocoa powder
- 2 large ripe avocados, peeled and diced

Directions

1. Merge all the ingredients into a food processor and process until smooth.
2. At some point while processing, stop the processor a couple of times to scrap the sides then re-start again to get a smoother consistency.
3. Move the pudding to a sealable container and keep it chilled for a few hours. Serve it with coconut whipped cream.

Nutrition:
Calories 76
Fat 4.3
Fiber 0.3
Carbs 2.2
Protein 7.4

205. Coffee Ice Cream

Preparation time: 10 minutes
Cooking time: 7 minutes
Servings: 8
Ingredients:

- 1/4 teaspoon stevia extract
- 1 teaspoon organic vanilla extract
- 2 tablespoons raw coconut nectar
- 1 cup organic coffee, double strength
- 1/4 teaspoon sea salt
- 2 teaspoons gelatin, unflavored
- 48 tablespoons organic coconut milk
- 1 oz. Kahlua

Directions

1. Add the organic coffee to a medium saucepan, and then simmer to reduce the amount to 1/2 cup.
2. Sprinkle gelatin on the coffee and then warm it over low heat, until the gelatin fully dissolves. You don't need to stir.
3. Spoon your coffee mixture into a blender, then blend until smooth. Add the coconut nectar, stevia and sea salt and continue to blend.
4. Add the vanilla, milk and Kahlua and continue to blend. Once done, pour in a glass container and cool for 6 hours while covered to get a custard-like substance.
5. Set to your ice cream maker and follow the manufacturer's instructions to make ice cream. Freeze for about 2 hours until it is firm.

Nutrition:
Calories 89
Fat 3.1
Fiber 2.8
Carbs 16.1
Protein 1.3

206. Banana Brownies

Preparation time: 15 minutes
Cooking time: 20 minutes
Servings: 16
Ingredients:

- A little ghee
- 1/2 cup semi-sweet dark chocolate chips
- 1/2 cup walnuts
- 11/2 cups rice flour
- 1/2 teaspoon baking powder
- 2 tablespoons cocoa powder, unsweetened
- 1 ounce soy protein powder or chocolate whey
- 1/2 cup almond milk
- 2 teaspoons vanilla extract
- 3/4 cup coconut sugar
- 1/4 cup sunflower oil
- 1 egg
- 1 cup ripe bananas, mashed; thawed, frozen

Directions

1. Use ghee to grease a baking pan or a 9×9 glass casserole dish as you preheat the oven to 350 degrees F.
2. Mix together the egg and mashed banana in a large bowl and then add in milk, vanilla, sugar and oil.
3. Also mix together baking powder, cocoa and milk protein powder in a small bowl and then blend in the dry mixture into the wet ingredients.
4. Stir in the flour, chocolate chips and walnuts until fully blended.
5. Pour the batter into a pan or dish, and bake in the preheated oven for 25-30 minutes. Once ready, cool in a pan and then cut into squares to serve.

Nutrition:
Calories 32
Fat 3.5
Fiber 0
Carbs 0.1
Protein 0

207. Vanilla Chia Pudding

Preparation time: 15 minutes
Cooking time: 20 minutes
Servings: 2
Ingredients:

- 1 teaspoon vanilla liquid stevia
- 1 teaspoon vanilla extract
- 1/3 cup chia seeds
- 1 cup almond milk, unsweetened
- Dairy-free whipped cream, optional

Directions

1. Combine and whisk the ingredients together and then pour into serving glasses.
2. Keep in the fridge for 10 minutes until set
3. If desired, set with some whipped cream and enjoy.

Nutrition:
Calories: 157.5 Fat: 3.8 g
Protein: 3 g Carbs: 32.3 g
Fiber: 4.5 g

208. Banana Pecan Ice Cream

Preparation time: 15 minutes
Cooking time: 20 minutes
Servings: 4
Ingredients:

- 1/2 cup pecans, chopped and toasted
- 1/2 cup canned coconut milk, chilled
- 3 tablespoons ghee
- 4 bananas

Directions

1. Slice 2 bananas and then put the slices into a sealed bag in the freezer for around 8 hours or precisely overnight
2. Also slice the 2 remaining bananas into rounds that are 1/2 an inch thick.
3. In a sauté pan, melt the ghee over medium or high heat.

4. Put the banana slices in the sauté pan and cook the mixture until the bananas turn golden brown. Flip the slices to make sure the other side has browned.

5. In a thick Ziploc bag or another container, pour the caramelized bananas and keep in the freezer for 8 hours or overnight.

6. Put all the 4 frozen bananas in a high-speed blender. Include both the caramelized and the un-caramelized bananas.

7. Pulse the frozen bananas to have them begin to appear like large bread crumbs, and then attach in the coconut milk and blend well. Keep scrapping down the sides and pressing the banana crumbles down to the center a number of times.

8. Blend until a smooth mixture is formed, of thick soft-serve ice cream consistency.

9. Add in the pecans to your ice cream and combine using a rubber spatula.

10. Once done, scoop into bowls and serve.

Nutrition:
Calories 32
Fat 3.5   Fiber 0
Carbs 0.1 Protein 0

209.   Pineapple Ice Cream

Preparation time: 15 minutes
Cooking time: 30 minutes
Servings: 6
Ingredients:
- 3 1/4 tablespoon activated black charcoal
- Small pinch of salt
- 1 teaspoon coconut extract
- 1 teaspoon vanilla extract
- 3/4 cup coconut sugar
- 1/2 cup almond milk
- 1 cup crushed pineapple
- 1 cup raw cashews, soaked 2 days and rinsed
- 2 cups full- fat coconut milk, chilled

Directions
1. Mix together almond milk and cashews in a high-speed blender and blend to obtain a thick and creamy consistency.
2. Attach in the rest of the ingredients apart from the pineapple and puree until smooth.
3. Transfer the ice cream to a bowl, whisk in pineapple and mix well. Attach the mixture

to the ice cream maker and follow the manufacturer's instructions to churn.

4. As soon as you obtain creamy frozen ice cream, serve or alternatively store in an airtight container. Keep it chilled to freeze fully.

Nutrition:
Calories 169 Fat 16.1
Fiber 2.8 Carbs 4.4 Protein 4.6

210. Fried Banana

Preparation time: 15 minutes
Cooking time: 20 minutes   Servings: 1
Ingredients:
- Olive oil or coconut oil
- A pinch of cinnamon
- 1 tablespoon organic honey
- 1 banana, sliced

Directions
1. Set a skillet, over medium heat, lightly drizzle the oil.
2. Arrange your banana slices in the skillet and cook for around 1-2 minutes on both sides.
3. As the banana slices cook, whisk a tablespoon of water and organic honey.
4. Detach the pan from heat and pour in your honey mixture over the sliced cooked bananas. Once cool, sprinkle with cinnamon and serve.

Nutrition:
Calories: 301
Fat: 9.3 g;
Protein: 6.8 g
Carbs: 49 g
Fiber: 1.9

CHAPTER 13

Conversion Tables

Volume Equivalents (Liquid)

US STANDARD	US STANDARD (OZ.)	METRIC (APPROXIMATE)
2 tbsp.	1 fl. oz.	30 mL
1/4 cup	2 fl. oz.	60 mL
1/2 cup	4 fl. oz.	120 mL
1 cup	8 fl. oz.	240 mL
11/2 cups	12 fl. oz.	355 mL
2 cups or 1 pint	16 fl. oz.	475 mL
4 cups or 1 quart	32 fl. oz.	1 L
1 gallon	128 fl. oz.	4 L

Volume Equivalents (Dry)

US STANDARD	METRIC (APPROXIMATE)
1/4 tsp.	1 mL
1/2 tsp.	2 mL
1 tsp.	5 mL
1 tbsp.	15 mL
1/4 cup	59 mL
cup	79 mL
1/2 cup	118 mL
1 cup	177 mL

Weight Equivalents

US STANDARD	METRIC (APPROXIMATE)
1/2 oz.	15 g
1 oz.	30 g
2 oz.	60 g

4 oz.	115 g
8 oz.	225 g
12 oz.	340 g
16 oz. or 1 lb.	455 g

Oven Temperatures

FAHRENHEIT (F)	CELSIUS (C) (APPROXIMATE)
250°F	120 °C
300°F	150°C
325°F	165°C
350°F	180°C
375°F	190°C
400°F	200°C
425°F	220°C
450°F	230°C

CHAPTER 14 - **30 Days Meal Plan**

Day 1

- Breakfast: Oatmeal with blueberries and almonds
- Snack: Greek yogurt with strawberries
- Lunch: Turkey and avocado wrap with carrot sticks
- Snack: Apple slices with peanut butter
- Dinner: Baked salmon with roasted vegetables

Day 2

- Breakfast: Scrambled eggs with spinach and whole wheat toast
- Snack: Cottage cheese with pineapple
- Lunch: Chicken and vegetable stir-fry with brown rice
- Snack: Baby carrots with hummus
- Dinner: Beef and vegetable kabobs with quinoa salad

Day 3

- Breakfast: Greek yogurt with granola and mixed berries
- Snack: Hard-boiled egg with cucumber slices
- Lunch: Turkey chili with whole wheat crackers
- Snack: Banana with almond butter
- Dinner: Grilled chicken breast with sweet potato fries and green beans

Day 4

- Breakfast: Smoothie with spinach, banana, and almond milk
- Snack: String cheese with apple slices
- Lunch: Tuna salad on whole wheat bread with cherry tomatoes
- Snack: Roasted almonds with dried apricots
- Dinner: Shrimp and vegetable stir-fry with brown rice

Day 5

- Breakfast: Whole wheat pancakes with mixed berries and honey
- Snack: Greek yogurt with honey and almonds
- Lunch: Vegetable and black bean quesadilla with salsa and avocado
- Snack: Grapes with cheese cubes
- Dinner: Grilled chicken breast with roasted vegetables and quinoa

Day 6

- Breakfast: Scrambled eggs with spinach and whole wheat toast
- Snack: Carrot sticks with hummus
- Lunch: Grilled chicken and vegetable kebab with quinoa salad

- Snack: Apple slices with peanut butter
- Dinner: Baked salmon with roasted vegetables

Day 7

- Breakfast: Greek yogurt with granola and mixed berries
- Snack: Hard-boiled egg with cucumber slices
- Lunch: Turkey and avocado wrap with carrot sticks
- Snack: Roasted almonds with dried apricots
- Dinner: Beef and vegetable kabobs with quinoa salad

Day 8

- Breakfast: Smoothie with spinach, banana, and almond milk
- Snack: String cheese with apple slices
- Lunch: Chicken and vegetable stir-fry with brown rice
- Snack: Banana with almond butter
- Dinner: Grilled chicken breast with sweet potato fries and green beans

Day 9

- Breakfast: Whole wheat pancakes with mixed berries and honey
- Snack: Cottage cheese with pineapple
- Lunch: Tuna salad on whole wheat bread with cherry tomatoes
- Snack: Baby carrots with hummus
- Dinner: Shrimp and vegetable stir-fry with brown rice

Day 10

- Breakfast: Oatmeal with blueberries and almonds
- Snack: Greek yogurt with strawberries
- Lunch: Vegetable and black bean quesadilla with salsa and avocado
- Snack: Grapes with cheese cubes
- Dinner: Baked salmon with roasted vegetables

Day 11

- Breakfast: Scrambled eggs with spinach and whole wheat toast
- Snack: Carrot sticks with hummus
- Lunch: Grilled chicken and vegetable kebab with quinoa salad
- Snack: Apple slices with peanut butter
- Dinner: Beef and vegetable kabobs with quinoa salad

Day 12

- Breakfast: Smoothie with spinach, banana, and almond milk
- Snack: String cheese with apple slices
- Lunch: Turkey chili with whole wheat crackers
- Snack: Roasted almonds with dried apricots
- Dinner: Grilled chicken breast with roasted vegetables and quinoa

Day 13

- Breakfast: Greek yogurt with fresh berries and granola.
- Snack: Apple slices with almond butter.
- Lunch: Grilled chicken salad with mixed greens, cherry tomatoes, cucumber, avocado, and balsamic vinaigrette.
- Snack: Carrot sticks with hummus.
- Dinner: Baked salmon with roasted asparagus and quinoa.

Day 14

- Breakfast: Whole grain toast with mashed avocado and a poached egg.
- Snack: Greek yogurt with sliced banana and honey.
- Lunch: Turkey wrap with spinach, tomato, avocado, and mustard on a whole wheat tortilla.
- Snack: Hard-boiled egg with sliced cucumber.
- Dinner: Beef stir-fry with broccoli, carrots, and brown rice.

Day 15

- Breakfast: Oatmeal with sliced almonds, banana, and cinnamon.
- Snack: Apple slices with cheddar cheese.
- Lunch: Grilled chicken Caesar salad with romaine lettuce, croutons, and parmesan cheese.
- Snack: Rice cakes with almond butter and banana slices.
- Dinner: Spaghetti squash with turkey meatballs and tomato sauce.

Day 16

- Breakfast: Green smoothie with spinach, banana, almond milk, and protein powder.
- Snack: Carrot sticks with tzatziki dip.
- Lunch: Quinoa salad with chickpeas, cucumber, tomato, and feta cheese.
- Snack: Greek yogurt with granola and berries.
- Dinner: Grilled shrimp skewers with roasted sweet potatoes and mixed vegetables.

Day 17

- Breakfast: Breakfast burrito with scrambled eggs, black beans, avocado, and salsa.
- Snack: Hard-boiled egg with cherry tomatoes.
- Lunch: Grilled chicken sandwich on whole grain bread with lettuce, tomato, and mustard.
- Snack: Cottage cheese with sliced peaches.
- Dinner: Baked cod with roasted Brussels sprouts and brown rice.

Day 18

- Breakfast: Overnight oats with sliced banana and peanut butter.
- Snack: Apple slices with cashew butter.
- Lunch: Tuna salad with mixed greens, cherry tomatoes, cucumber, and balsamic vinaigrette.
- Snack: Greek yogurt with sliced strawberries.
- Dinner: Turkey chili with mixed vegetables and a side salad.

Day 19

- Breakfast: Whole grain toast with scrambled eggs and sliced avocado.
- Snack: Rice cakes with almond butter and sliced apple.
- Lunch: Grilled chicken Caesar wrap with romaine lettuce, croutons, and parmesan cheese on a whole wheat tortilla.
- Snack: Carrot sticks with hummus.
- Dinner: Beef and vegetable stir-fry with brown rice.

Day 20

- Breakfast: Greek yogurt with sliced banana and chopped nuts.
- Snack: Hard-boiled egg with sliced cucumber.
- Lunch: Turkey and cheese sandwich on whole grain bread with lettuce, tomato, and mustard.
- Snack: Cottage cheese with sliced peaches.
- Dinner: Baked salmon with roasted Brussels sprouts and quinoa.

Day 21

- Breakfast: Omelette with spinach, mushroom, and feta cheese.
- Snack: Apple slices with almond butter.
- Lunch: Quinoa salad with grilled chicken, mixed greens, cherry tomatoes, and balsamic vinaigrette.
- Snack: Greek yogurt with granola and berries.
- Dinner: Chicken fajitas with peppers and onions on whole wheat tortillas.

Day 22:

- Breakfast: Greek yogurt with fresh berries and a sprinkle of granola.
- Snack: Sliced cucumber with hummus.
- Lunch: Grilled chicken breast with roasted vegetables (zucchini, bell peppers, and eggplant).
- Snack: Apple slices with almond butter.
- Dinner: Baked salmon with garlic and herb butter, served with steamed broccoli and quinoa.

Day 23:

- Breakfast: Veggie omelet with spinach, cherry tomatoes, and feta cheese.
- Snack: Baby carrots with ranch dressing.
- Lunch: Tuna salad with mixed greens, cucumber, and cherry tomatoes.
- Snack: Greek yogurt with honey and sliced almonds.
- Dinner: Pork tenderloin with sweet potato wedges and sautéed kale.

Day 24:

- Breakfast: Smoothie bowl with mixed berries, banana, Greek yogurt, and granola.
- Snack: Sliced bell pepper with hummus.
- Lunch: Grilled chicken salad with mixed greens, avocado, and cherry tomatoes.
- Snack: Hard-boiled egg.
- Dinner: Baked chicken thighs with roasted root vegetables (carrots, parsnips, and sweet potatoes).

Day 25:

- Breakfast: Scrambled eggs with sliced avocado and whole grain toast.
- Snack: Apple slices with peanut butter.
- Lunch: Turkey and cheese sandwich on whole grain bread with sliced cucumber and carrot sticks.
- Snack: Greek yogurt with fresh berries.
- Dinner: Beef stir-fry with mixed vegetables (broccoli, snap peas, bell peppers, and onion) served with brown rice.

Day 26:

- Breakfast: Breakfast burrito with scrambled eggs, black beans, avocado, and salsa wrapped in a whole wheat tortilla.
- Snack: Sliced mango.
- Lunch: Grilled chicken with roasted Brussels sprouts and sweet potato mash.
- Snack: Hard-boiled egg.
- Dinner: Grilled shrimp skewers with mixed vegetables (zucchini, onion, and bell pepper) and quinoa.

Day 27:

- Breakfast: Overnight oats with almond milk, chia seeds, sliced banana, and chopped walnuts.
- Snack: Sliced bell pepper with hummus.
- Lunch: Tuna salad with mixed greens, cherry tomatoes, and cucumber.
- Snack: Greek yogurt with honey and sliced almonds.
- Dinner: Baked salmon with roasted asparagus and brown rice.

Day 28:

- Breakfast: Veggie frittata with mixed peppers, onion, and zucchini.
- Snack: Sliced cucumber with ranch dressing.
- Lunch: Grilled chicken salad with mixed greens, cherry tomatoes, and avocado.
- Snack: Hard-boiled egg.
- Dinner: Beef chili with mixed beans, served with a side of cornbread.

Day 29:

- Breakfast: Smoothie with mixed berries, banana, Greek yogurt, and spinach.
- Snack: Sliced apple with peanut butter.
- Lunch: Grilled chicken with roasted sweet potatoes and green beans.
- Snack: Baby carrots with hummus.
- Dinner: Baked cod with lemon and herb seasoning, served with steamed broccoli and quinoa.

Day 30:

- Breakfast: Greek yogurt with sliced banana and chopped walnuts.
- Snack: Sliced bell pepper with hummus.
- Lunch: Turkey and cheese wrap with mixed greens, cherry tomatoes, and sliced avocado.
- Snack: Hard-boiled egg.
- Dinner: Pork chops with roasted carrots and green beans

Note: This meal plan is just an example and can be modified based on individual preferences and dietary restrictions.

Conclusion

The Paleo diet is a lifestyle answer that has been steadily gaining popularity these days. Many people are finding this diet very beneficial to their health. It is a natural diet that focuses on whole, unprocessed foods.

With the Paleo diet, you can lose weight and feel healthier. The Paleo diet is low in sugar. It is free of grains, dairy products, legumes, refined carbohydrates, and processed foods. This means that you get to eat natural foods rich in vitamins, minerals, antioxidants, and fiber.

The Paleo diet helps in the prevention of various diseases. Some of the Paleo diet benefits include an improved immune system and a reduction of chances of developing certain kinds of cancer and heart disease. This paleo diet is a manner of eating that became popular in the early 2000s. It's a lifestyle that hunter-gatherers have practiced for millions of years before the advent of agriculture. One of the main ideas behind this is that we are evolved to eat foods that are in season at the time. It's a way to ensure we get nutrients from our food. A straightforward way to implement this way of eating is to find whole, fresh foods that are in season at the time. The paleo diet doesn't encourage consuming processed foods, fast food, or refined sugars or oils. It's considered ideal for keeping your mind and body healthy. It's also great for weight loss since it encourages eating fresh foods and minimizes your exposure to chemicals such as preservatives and artificial additives. The paleo diet is a lifestyle of Paleolithic humans. This means that the way they ate was different from the way we eat today. This diet was designed as a way to mimic our ancestor's eating habits.

The paleo diet is a center point on eating foods that are rich in vitamins and minerals. These foods include fish, meats, vegetables, fruits, nuts, and seeds. This diet also encourages low glycemic fruits and vegetables that are low on the glycemic index.

As beneficial as this diet may be to your health, it also has drawbacks. For example- individuals following the paleo diet can suffer from nutrient deficiencies. This type of diet can also lead to a greater incidence of health issues like acne and cancer.

However, you cope with these issues, you should know about what the paleo diet is and how it's used today.

Made in the USA
Las Vegas, NV
04 October 2023

78440619R10068